MW00561418

WHAT PEOPLE ARE SAYING ABOUT
STOP SETTLING...

Rick is one of the most caring people I have ever met and his road from struggle to significance an inspiration to us all. If you want to learn about turning adversity into success in all areas of life this is the book for you. It's both compelling and practical. Rick is one of the few folks I have ever known who has built wealth and then used it to really help others.

Bob Kilinski
Southeast Regional Owner, Keller Williams Realty

Visionary and practical. I'm not sure those two words describe very many books, but they certainly do for Rick Hale's *Stop Settling.* Rick gently pushes us to aim higher—far higher—to make a difference in the lives of others, no matter what career path we're on. And he provides brass tacks, hands-on tools to help us make (and keep) commitments that will lead to a fulfilling, meaningful life. When you read this book, you'll be both challenged and encouraged.

David Osborn
NYT best-selling author of *Wealth Can't Wait,*
***Tribe of Millionaires, Bidding to Buy* and**
Miracle Morning Millionaires

Like a great coach or mentor, Rick weaves timeless truths into his personal story and draws from the inspiration of others. The result is that you will be challenged to lay aside your excuses and be renewed in a vision to bring your best self to every occasion.

Dr. Randy Ross
CEO of Remarkable!, best-selling author and craftsman of
Culture & Hope

I appreciate authors who can distill a wealth of wisdom into bite-size morsels. In *Stop Settling,* Rick Hale paints a broad picture of purpose and motivation, and then he brings it down into daily decisions that gradually fulfill our highest goals. Read this book. It'll make a difference.

Hal Elrod
International keynote speaker and best-selling author of
The Miracle Morning **and** *The Miracle Equation*

Rick Hale has given the world a powerful personal message about rejection, recovery, and forgiveness, leading to his ultimate and amazing success. You will be engaged, you will be moved emotionally, and you will be inspired to become "your best" You!

Kay Evans
Co-owner, Southeast Region Keller Williams Realty

Within one week of meeting Rick Hale over 20 years ago and hearing of his journey, I began encouraging him to write his book: "People NEED to hear your story." Rick's story has and will change many lives. Buried in it is a blueprint for life that's clarifying and easy to follow. Simply put, it's an inspiring recipe for exposing your ultimate best.

Rami F. Odeh
Author of *Quiet The Noise: A Trail Runners' Path To Hearing God*

I've been fortunate to have played alongside Rick Hale for 25 years in building one of the most successful real estate brands in the country. He is genuine, smart, and talented. He is collaborative and he always comes from contribution. He is unequivocally the nicest, kindest, most successful person I know. Oh, and he has become wealthy all the while I've known him. I say all of this because *Stop Settling* proves all of it. It's all in here. The authenticity, the intelligence, the talent, the collaboration, the contribution, the kindness, and the success. All of it. You'd be crazy or stupid not to read it, learn from it and put his efforts to improve your life to work for yourself as soon as possible. I, for one, will be referencing this book for many, many years to come. Thank you, Rick! You are a gift, and so is this book!

Shaun Rawls

Author, founder and CEO of Rawls Consulting

STOP SETTLING

FINDING CLEAR DIRECTIONS FOR A REGRET-FREE LIFE

RICK HALE

Cover design and interior formatting by Anne McLaughlin, Blue Lake Design.

ISBNs:
Hardcover Print: 978-1-951022-24-2
Digital: 978-1-951022-27-3

First printing 2023

Published by Rick Hale Leadership, Atlanta, Georgia

Printed in the United States of America

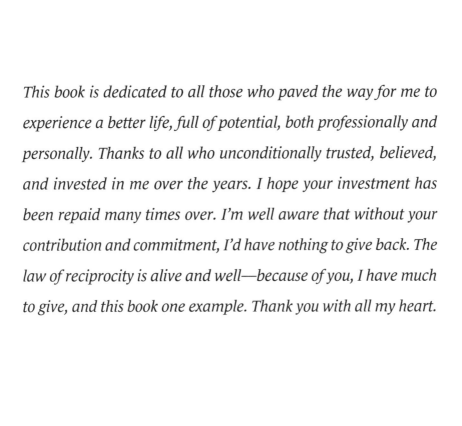

This book is dedicated to all those who paved the way for me to experience a better life, full of potential, both professionally and personally. Thanks to all who unconditionally trusted, believed, and invested in me over the years. I hope your investment has been repaid many times over. I'm well aware that without your contribution and commitment, I'd have nothing to give back. The law of reciprocity is alive and well—because of you, I have much to give, and this book one example. Thank you with all my heart.

TABLE OF CONTENTS

INTRODUCTION

"Son, you have a distinct lack of failure in your life."

I could tell my stepfather's comment wasn't intended as a compliment, and I was confused. Wasn't a lack of failure supposed to be a *good* thing? I couldn't believe he could say that to me. I immediately became defensive and began to list reasons in my mind why he was wrong.

How could he insinuate that I was unsuccessful? At age twenty-six, I had already checked off many of my lifetime goals:

- Business degree from Georgia State University;

- Decent job with several years' experience so far;

- Nice salary;

- 401(k) plan in place;

- Home ownership;

- Ample proof of coolness (Jeep, sports car, motorcycle, etc.); and

- Making original rock n' roll music in a band on the side.

I wasn't just successful at work; I could boast a lot of factors I felt were somewhat cool and that many of my peers still dreamed of. But the more I thought about it, I realized my stepfather wasn't discounting those accomplishments. He simply had observed that I wasn't fulfilling my potential—that my lack of risk-taking was holding me back.

I reluctantly took a closer look at my life and saw that he was right. My work allowed me to live comfortably, but it was not remotely inspiring or exciting. As my twenties came to an end, I knew I couldn't do it anymore. I had to confess that I didn't want my boss's job . . . or his boss's job . . . or, frankly, any job in the company.

I felt the need to breathe, grow, and do something big. My stepfather was right. I wasn't growing because I wasn't taking any real chances. I certainly don't remember saying, "Life is short; I think I'll shoot for a 6 or 7 out of 10 and call it a day," yet that's essentially what I was doing, even if my idea of a 7 was someone else's 8 or 9. What matters is owning your true potential and how you see yourself, not looking at yourself through the lens of someone else.

Bottom line: I wasn't fully alive. And isn't that the goal of a life well lived and worth living? I was traveling in slow motion, miles from my potential as a child of God, a God I believed to be all-powerful. I still think God wants us to deep dive and explore our true potential, not merely skim the surface. I was skimming along better than most, but still wading in the shallow end of life.

Fast-forward a couple of decades to my family's annual snowboarding trip out west, at the peak of Whistler Mountain in British Columbia, Canada. I found a place where the snow was soft and fresh, far away from the chaos of the ski lift and typical ski traffic. I detached my boots from my snowboard and just laid back in the snow, looking at the magnificent panoramic vistas and feeling the warm sunshine and soft, cool breeze on my face.

Immersed in the sights and sounds of nature, I was keenly aware of how big the planet is, how big God is, and what a small player I am in the big picture. Here, on the mountain, I had no meetings to attend, no cellphone in my pocket, no to-do list hijacking my sacred thoughts. I thought, *This is why I made the trip!* Among my other thoughts that day, I recalled my stepfather's words and felt immense gratitude that he had cared enough to challenge me about my "distinct lack of failure."

I had almost settled for a safe and predictable life of comfort and success—but my definition of *success* was far different then from what it has since become. Then, it had been having enough to coast through life. Now it is the ability to feel fully alive, whether I'm snowboarding on a majestic mountain or going through a routine workday. Success is no longer simply a life of financial freedom; now it includes mental clarity, a sense of purpose, and a persistent feeling of contentment with my family, my work, and myself.

My purpose for writing this book is to inspire others, just as others have inspired me along this journey called life, to embrace a life filled with ups and downs, setbacks and crises, even rejection and failure— to stay positive and move forward even when life and people let you down. When quitting seems the simplest (and most logical) option, you simply don't quit.

I don't mind making mistakes; that's how we learn and grow. But I don't want to have any regrets when the last bell rings and my last breath leaves my lungs. I don't think you do, either. At twenty-six, I had been playing it safe. If that had continued, it would have been my life's biggest regret. It has been far better to embrace the many mistakes and lessons learned as I've worked to create a more fulfilling, more exciting, more abundant life.

Success begins with hard work, of course. Through persistence, risk, and (yes) occasional failure, I have accumulated an interest in twenty-plus privately held companies, each that create a return for me and allow me to work because I want to, not because I have to. I love my work, but I work because it creates margin for the *other* things I love. Even when I'm in the trenches working full tilt, I try to make time to road and mountain bike, ride motocross, wake-surf and wakeboard, snowboard, fish, scuba dive off of topical islands, and even skydive on occasion. In my forties I discovered the joy of painting, and now I paint for personal enjoyment and to donate my art to charity and friends. I collect guitars and play almost daily, often performing with other musicians.

I am also committed to help at-risk teens find a better path, one that is healthy and empowering. The goal is to reach them before they make decisions that aren't reversible—to plant positive seeds now that lead to a fulfilling life later. I'm able to support numerous organizations that impact youth, thanks to my hard work and good fortune, and because I created a plan to support that goal personally.

It's not my intent to boast of my accomplishments or lifestyle. I'm certain my story pales in comparison to what others have overcome and achieved. Yet I've been inspired by so many other people's stories (many of whom I will be quoting throughout this book), and I hope my own story will inspire you. I want my four boys, their children to be born someday, and everyone else who is willing to work at it, to stop settling and learn to live a regret-free life.

Throughout this book, I will be encouraging you to make some bold choices, and to make them at points in your life when they matter most. Choice equals real freedom, and freedom is the pinnacle jumping-off point for joy.

How would it feel to have a life where you were swimming with the current and not against it each day? What if others weren't in control of your potential and your pursuit of the things that make your heart sing? What if you could regularly enjoy travel, art, mission work, philanthropy, and all your other favorite activities without waiting until retirement? What if you could maintain such a lifestyle and still leave a financially sound, self-sustaining legacy for your family members and favorite charities? These are choices I will be asking you to consider, and I'll help you see how to get from where you are now to where you want to be.

Successful author and coach (and good friend of mine), Eric Saperston, once told me that he had discovered a key difference between those who succeed at a high level and those who don't: a willingness to ask for help. Those who ask for help find ways to rise above all the obstacles and hiccups they face. Those who don't are limited to their own natural abilities (as strong as they might be) and miss the benefit of others' experience, role modeling, and wise counsel. A question unasked is a question unanswered . . . and a question unanswered could the one that keeps you from your fullest potential.

Eric has credibility in asking penetrating questions. He is the director and lead actor in the movie, *The Journey,* which is a remake of his own remarkable path. After college, he bought a Volkswagen bus and followed the tour of the Grateful Dead with his dog Jack. At his father's suggestion, as he traveled the country, he invited some very famous and influential people to have a cup of coffee with him. Before long, three others joined him on the trek from Atlanta to Seattle, asking life's most challenging questions and discovering some amazing answers. His experience is summed up in his statement: "Sometimes you take a trip. Sometimes the trip takes you!" He asks, "Are you on a journey leading you somewhere you choose to go, and are you armed with high level questions along the way that elevate your experience?" I love another question he asks: "Do you wake up excited and go to bed fulfilled?" Let me ask, if not, why not? What would it look like to achieve that goal? Remember, you get one run at it. It's not a dress rehearsal.

The advent of the United States Global Positioning System (GPS) virtually eliminated the need for physical maps. Based on what I see and read, users have almost unanimously made it clear that GPS is not just a source, but the source for determining how to arrive where they're intending to go. It even calculates trends in traffic flow and identifies accidents in real time—and it redirects us within seconds to find a better route. Amazing!

Planning—in any area, but especially when we're charting our best future—is like using the GPS on the phone or the dash of our cars. We enter the data of where we are and where we want to go, and the satellites and terabytes go to work to give us the best route to get there. The program steers us around traffic delays, wrecks, and road construction so we get to our destination as quickly and smoothly as possible. It's an awesome tool! In our life planning, however, the satellites are different; we tap into the wisdom of mentors, authors, and friends who give us plenty of input and feedback—similar to the kind of input and feedback Waze or Google Maps gets from other cars on the streets and highways. With this information, we chart our course, pick the best route, and avoid most (but not all) of the roadblocks along the way. That's how we find and follow our path to our best life, and that's what this book is all about.

There's no rule that says it takes a lifetime, or even years, to begin to realize your improved life. It's up to the goals you set, the effort you put into it, and the persistence you show when luck doesn't seem to be going your way.

Let me also give you a spoiler alert up front: the real benefit of financial freedom is in the relationships you build and add value to. If my primary focus ever appears to be on financial gain, it's not. I've met many immensely wealthy people who were some of the most miserable people I've ever seen! I think most of us want to be around others who love us not for our wealth and resources, but because of shared interests and genuine concern for one another.

Okay. It's almost time to get started. I'm going to begin with a little of my personal background to demonstrate that success is definitely not determined (or limited) by someone's upbringing. Then we'll move on to a lot of practical lessons and applications. But first, I want to point to a scene in a movie that's both funny and fundamental.

I like a scene from the movie *We're the Millers*, a comedy about a family on the road. At one stop, the teenage girl arranges a date with a rough-looking street punk. When he comes to pick her up, a bold tattoo is clearly visible across his upper chest, right below his necklace. It reads, "NO RAGRETS." The girl's dad asks him about it, and the kid explains, "That's my credo: No regrets."

The dad replies, "You have no regrets? Not even a single letter?"

Even though we may come to "ragret" some of our mistakes, let's never confuse mistakes with regrets. Regrets are lifelong disappointments most of us see as irrevocable, but mistakes are a natural part of everyone's journey toward success. If we overcome our fear and reluctance, we discover our mistakes result in helping us become better people.

CHAPTER 1

YOUR PAST DOES NOT DETERMINE YOUR FUTURE

Recently, I was speaking to a group of sales professionals and asked them to think of their fifty-year-future selves. I asked, "What would need to happen for you to be able to say, thirty, forty, or fifty years from today, 'My life was regret-free and awesome!'?"

You should have seen the looks on their faces. You could tell the very thought was inconceivable to most of them. They could barely fathom it. Some tried to explain to me that they were simply too busy just trying to get through the day, get through the week, and hopefully make it to the weekend without too much trauma. For most, taking time to really think big fits nowhere into that paradigm.

I wonder what percentage of the workers in our country lives for the six-pack and ballgame on the weekend. How many of us settle for a job that robs us of energy rather than fueling our passion, vision, and overall contribution to the world? Are you working in a job where your primary goal is to survive until Friday at 5:00 p.m.? Do you feel relief when the workweek is over, then get stressed-out on Sunday night before jumping back on the proverbial treadmill of life?

American workers aren't very good at planning. We fail to look ahead to potential options and outcomes, and we don't understand how to set a productive pace for ourselves. After coaching hundreds of professionals, I've seen that most of them overestimate what they can do in one year and vastly underestimate how much they can do in five years. Few if any have dared consider what they might accomplish in fifty years. They set meager (they tend to say "reasonable") goals, year after year—or worse, they set goals they don't believe in, hit reset the next New Year, fail again, and the cycle continues. But what might happen if we dared to set our sights on a goal that would take decades rather than months to accomplish?

THE POWER OF 10,000 HOURS

In his book, *Outliers,* Malcolm Gladwell researched top-tier elite athletes, musicians, and performers. He wanted to discover what set them apart from those that were merely good. He cited a study from the early 1990s at a Berlin music school. The school's violinists were separated into three groups: (1) students with the potential to become world-class soloists; (2) those judged to be merely "good" at a professional level; and (3) those who were unlikely to ever play professionally and intended to become public school music teachers. All students were asked, "Over the course of your entire career, ever since you first picked up the violin, how many hours have you practiced?" Here was the study's conclusion:

Everyone from all three groups started playing at roughly the same age, around five years old. In those first few years, everyone practiced roughly the same amount, about two or three hours a week. But when the students were around the age of eight, real differences started to emerge. The students who would end up the best in their class began to practice more than everyone else: six hours a week by age nine, eight hours a week by age twelve, sixteen hours a week by age fourteen, and up and up, until by the age of twenty they were practicing—that is, purposefully and single-mindedly playing their instruments with the intent to get better—well over thirty hours a week. In fact, by the age of twenty, the elite performers had each totaled ten thousand hours of practice. By contrast, the merely good students had totaled eight thousand hours, and the future music teachers had totaled just over four thousand hours."

A follow-up study with pianists revealed the same pattern. Gladwell then demonstrated how "the 10,000-hour rule" also held true for professional hockey, soccer, computer programming, and even the success of the Beatles and Bill Gates.

Does the 10,000-hour rule also apply to business? I am convinced it does. Someone willing to devote that much time working on a passionate pursuit tends to become best in class. They become invaluable and irreplaceable to their employers. Few if any can compete at that level, and those who do can command the price they feel is justified for their performance.

Even better, what if you're best in class and are pouring that level of passion and interest into your own company? Best in class always attracts phenomenal talent. People want to learn from the best, which is why winners are so hard to dethrone. Consider what Nick Saban has done at the University of Alabama, or Bill Belichick with the New England Patriots. They improve their team's record to the point where it's assumed and expected that they win—and then all the players and fans adopt that attitude. The expectation that you're supposed to win is a real difference maker.

To be the best in a field, you must think long-term. Most people tend to gauge success based on the model on the left (below). They expect to see regular (linear) improvement, even if such gains are modest. Long-term thinkers, however, follow a model that looks more like a hockey stick. Growth and profit may remain flat for a time, but eventually will spike and then increase very quickly. Delayed results aren't unusual for those hoping to achieve significant and relevant outcomes in their lives. Most people are quick to panic and bail out when they don't see immediate success. They'll initiate a new endeavor or change in behavior, but then quit too soon and turn their attention to something else.

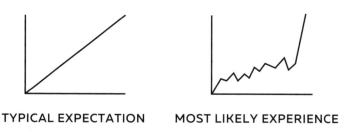

TYPICAL EXPECTATION   **MOST LIKELY EXPERIENCE**

Short-term thinking is the norm, which is a primary reason why big success is so rare. I can attest that eighty percent of those in the real estate industry earn a modest income, typically below $40,000 per year. Another fifteen percent averages closer to $100,000 per year. But the top five percent often earn over $500,000 annually, with the top one percent bringing in multi-millions. It definitely isn't a linear gain in income.

I'm convinced that if only a small number of people really began to think big, it could change the world. If just a few of us begin to tap into why we are here and what drives us, we can lead the way. I hope I can convince you to get out of survival mode and discover a brand-new way of life. Enduring repetitive five-day chunks of life at a time and living for the weekend is a pattern so prevalent that many workers accept it as inevitable. I encourage you to plan for the long run, put in the hours to master your chosen craft, and reap the rewards.

Simply put, do you want to be part of the seventy percent who settle and scrape by, the twenty-five percent who do pretty well and have a decent life and fairly predictable shot at a secure retirement, or the five percent who absolutely crush it and script the outcome they choose? You can be in that select group if you develop a compelling vision, an effective strategy, and a workable plan. Keep reading, I'm certain the answer will come to you.

GETTING PAST YOUR PAST

As we've seen, a lot of people never achieve the best in life because they're too quick to abandon reasonable long-term goals and settle for paltry progress. As they shift from one short-term goal to another, they never come close to putting in their 10,000 hours and becoming truly proficient at anything.

Another common roadblock to success is failure to deal with mental limitations that are ingrained on us during childhood. I recently read that seventy percent of all adults repeat the experiences and lifestyle they were exposed to as a child. That may not sound like anything to be concerned about if you had a happy and healthy childhood. But as I've gotten older and after coaching hundreds of people, I'm seeing that such ideal childhoods appear to be extremely rare. While I would never dispute that childhood programming has significant potential to impact adult perception and behavior, I'm here to tell you it doesn't have to.

No experience is permanent unless you allow it to be. Why do we so quickly accept that failure or other unpleasant experiences are permanent? Throughout this book you'll hear many references to the power of taking negative situations and converting them to positives. We need to realize that all those black clouds of life have silver linings. That's the only way to stay empowered and positive in the face of setbacks.

So what if seventy percent of the population lives an inferior life where potential is never realized? That's for them to reconcile. What happens in your life is up to you. Why wouldn't you look in the mirror and state with confidence and absolute conviction: *I am worthy. I am in the thirty percent that has chosen to own my destiny?*

IF IT'S TO BE, WHY NOT ME?

Choice, not chance, determines your destiny. But choice requires crafting a plan, trusting the plan, and doing the work required to reach each milestone along the way leading to your desired outcome.

Your past does not determine your future. You can do nothing to change your past, but your future is entirely up to you. Regardless of any disappointments or detrimental events in your childhood, you can now make new plans, form new relationships, live new places. It's all up to you now. Such freedom of choice may feel overwhelming at first, but stick to your new mindset, supported by awareness and steady effort. You'll eventually feel a tailwind, and ongoing progress becomes easier.

Success breeds success, but step one is the most important. There is no progression or step two without a first step, right?

Take it from me. I wasn't, as they say, "born on third base, thinking I hit a triple." Many people—Americans especially—seem to think that a certain level of privilege is a real advantage, if not a requirement, for success. I don't agree. In fact, I think that the first step to success is the ability to see life clearly, properly assess where you are now and where you'd like to be, and plan the most effective path to get you there. I suspect that privilege often impedes the ability to see clearly and plan accordingly.

If you'll bear with me, I'd like to quickly share my story to assure you that I didn't get a lot of head-starts to a successful and satisfying life. After I give you my background, believe me, the rest of the book will be about you.

MY STORY

I was born in the charity ward of a hospital in Augusta, Georgia. My mother had been so afraid of her tyrannical father that she ran off to school in Austria, where she met my father while in line registering for her first classes, which led to their first date. Unexpectedly, she almost immediately got pregnant with me, and they decided to get married to "do the right thing." In a foreign country and in a panic at age nineteen, she convinced her new husband to move to Augusta, Georgia. My mother was very unhappy in the relationship, and the marriage ended before I turned two. A few years later, thanks to an abundance of grit and determination, my father finished medical school, even though he had no local family for moral or economic support, and he moved on to New York to complete his residency. Mom moved the two of us to Athens, Georgia, to stay with her parents. She remarried a few years later.

During his last year of medical school, my dad struggled to make ends meet and was unable to pay child support. Mom decided to play hardball, giving him the options of an unforgiving legal system, paying all he owed in back child support, or forfeiting me for adoption. He reluctantly allowed my stepfather to adopt me, a decision he would later regret.

The next five years were filled with good memories. Mom had another child—my new brother, Eric. We felt like a solid, prototypical family, even though we moved four times during that period. Since both my parents were working, Eric and I spent a lot of time with all-day babysitters before I started school fulltime. One of them had a teenage son who treated me like his little brother and initiated my lifelong love for music, beginning with my first 45 rpm record: "Joy to the World" by Three Dog Night. But more on that later.

At six years old, I contracted pneumonia and simultaneously suffered kidney failure. The local hospital couldn't help, so I was rushed to Duke University Hospital where they decided it best to remove my right kidney. At the time, the surgery required being cut open, stomach to back, which left an enormous scar wrapping most of my hip and side. The silver lining was that I became popular as I entertained kids on the playground with what I called my pet: a "two-foot fat worm" wrapped around my hip. Thankfully, the scar has faded and thinned over the years, but it's still a reminder that health is not to be taken for granted.

When I was ten, two announcements from my parents destroyed the security of my childhood. My dad (I had not yet been told that he was really my stepfather) told me that he was divorcing my mom because he was in love with our neighbor across the street. She had been a close friend of my mom's, and I was friends with her kids. To further complicate the situation, she was divorcing her husband at the same time to marry my dad.

It was a lot for a ten-year-old mind to absorb, but the shock was not yet over. My mother then told me, "I love you very much, but I have cancer. You and your brother Eric can stay with me or go live with your father—it's your choice, and we don't want to separate you. But if you stay with me, you should know that it'll be rough and I won't be able to care for you as I should." To say that I felt tremendous distress and pressure would be an understatement.

I didn't want to make either choice—a decision no ten-year-old should ever have to make, but I finally opted to live with my father, new stepmother, brother, and her young son and daughter. The new arrangement started out fine, but then Dad started working many nights, leaving my stepmom to care for four kids between five and ten years old. It became too much for her to handle. Since I wasn't either of theirs by birth or blood, they started looking for other options for me. Going back to my mom wasn't an option because she had moved to Venezuela. I visited her when I was eleven and overheard a phone call she had with my adoptive father and stepmother after I had worn out my welcome with them. They said, "We just think Ricky is more than we can handle. He's unruly, and we can't manage him. He is really your responsibility and we don't want him here anymore." They proceeded to list everything they thought was wrong with me and why I simply didn't fit into their lives. They then announced that my mother, living in Venezuela, should take custody.

But they also posed a solution: "We have found a military school in Florida. Maybe that will fix him." Mom agreed to send me there.

Four decades later, that phone call is still clear in my mind. It remains one of the most damaging memories of my childhood, primarily because it initiated the loneliest year I have ever endured. The school they sent me to, near Fort Lauderdale, was filled with kids from primarily wealthy but dysfunctional homes where the adults were satisfied to let the school do their parenting for them. Other students had been sent from Latin America to get a U.S. education. Tuition was expensive, and how my mom afforded it was beyond me, but it was a terrible investment, in my opinion.

I cried myself to sleep every night for the first few weeks of my sixth-grade experience until, eventually, I began to adjust to my new world. Adapting to the diverse mix of personalities was the hardest challenge I'd ever faced, but I grew tougher and learned to make friends.

I discovered I was good at team sports, and I listened to music as an escape. I found an abandoned pair of drumsticks and learned to play beats on every available hard surface, channeling my hyperactive energy into a productive outlet as I thought about happier places.

By this time, I'd learned about my biological father, and was thrilled when he dropped in with his wonderful wife to visit me. We connected almost immediately. I even went to see them in New York during a school break and got to meet my sister, Summer. I was delighted when they invited me to live with them, but my mother vetoed that idea. I see now that it was a matter of pride: she had no intention of moving back to the States, but I was her responsibility and she wanted to prove she had her life under control again.

I was disappointed, of course, but my life still took a turn for the better. Mom started dating a businessman who worked setting up offshore corporations for international trade. I met him while visiting her on the Caribbean island of Aruba, off the coast of Venezuela, where she was temporarily working as a lab technician for the Pan-American Health Organization. She was putting in longer hours than he did, so he kept me entertained with daily adventures, exploring and having fun—experiences that were very different from my encounters with other father figures.

He taught me to water ski in the ocean, sparking the beginning of my love of boating and water sports. He taught me how to drive a stick shift in his Toyota Starlet rental car, and within a couple days I was navigating the streets of the small island as an unlicensed driver. Thanks to his attention during that break, I returned to military school feeling empowered, and in fact, like an adult for the first time. I was beginning to believe in myself and, for better or worse, adopted the mindset that breaking some rules is just fine if no one gets hurt along the way!

In fact, I was more motivated than ever to succeed. My new potential stepfather had invited me to move to Massachusetts and live with him and his parents when I got out of school, but he had one condition: I had to stay out of trouble and make good grades. He didn't need to ask twice. Anything was better than another year in military school. After being a complete academic failure for the first half, I finished the year a top cadet with straight A's and many honors, including the prestigious Cadet of the Month award. It's amazing what a little motivation will do in a young boy's life. I also discovered that I was very competitive and liked a good challenge with a reward attached.

When my sixth-grade year was over, I made the move north. Mom was planning to join us as soon as she finished some work in Aruba, an island off the coast of Venezuela. I lived with my new potential stepfather in Massachusetts for two years, sometimes traveling with him on business trips to various cities and foreign countries, including a safari into the backwoods of Surname. What an adventure at a young age to see how the rest of the world lives! But back home in Massachusetts, for the first time in my life, I felt completely wanted and loved. Simply being back in a real home with a real family was such a relief at that point in my life. And when my school commitments prevented me from traveling with him, I stayed with his parents at their farmhouse in a small rural Massachusetts community. During that time I took up playing the trombone and joined the stage band during middle school. It was a happy and memorable time in my life. I fondly remember Friday fish fries, a newfound love of clams from a local restaurant, and playing the classic card game Old Maid with his parents, whom I affectionately called Gram and Gramps. They were wonderful people, and I miss them still today. It was a glimpse of normalcy I desperately needed at a critical time in my life.

For some reason, my mother never made it to Massachusetts. I suspect she knew something I hadn't yet discovered. I got a clue on one trip I took with my potential stepfather. We were on the way home from one of the Caribbean islands with something like $25,000 in cash, and he had me carry $5,000—the maximum amount that wasn't required to be disclosed at customs. At the time, I felt like I'd gotten a good start on my new desire to become an entrepreneurial success story and make enough money to control my own life. My newest self-appointed father figure was quick to remind me that money is worthless without great people in your life—a lesson I've never forgotten. But what he neglected to tell me was that his laxity with handling Uncle Sam's money was becoming a very real problem for him . . . and would ultimately affect me.

It wasn't long before he was convicted of various financial crimes. I was flown back to Georgia to spend a month or so with my grandparents, and when he was sentenced to four years in prison, the stay with my grandparents became permanent. Another change. Another school. Another challenge to make new friends. My family in Massachusetts never forwarded my personal belongings. I'd like to think they were hoping I would eventually return. I did, but it was many years later when I went for a visit while in college. In the meantime, all I had was in a suitcase packed for a short-term visit as I began yet another "start over."

By now I had begun to develop a knack for finding the positive side of even not-so-great circumstances. I was older, and more self-confident. I was in Athens, home of the University of Georgia and the Bulldogs, the greatest football program in the world (according to most of the residents). I strategically shortened my name from Ricky to "Rick" as I began a year in yet another new school, and I was determined to make the new "Rick" much cooler than the old "Ricky" ever was.

Yet this transition to living with my grandparents proved to be more difficult than I had anticipated. To the outside world, my grandfather appeared to be an inspiring success story. At nineteen, he and my grandmother had fled from the communist regime in Europe with only one suitcase between the two of them. They were in a train station in Munich, Germany, in the 1940s as allied troops attacked from the air. While they were running through the railyard to escape danger, a bomb struck nearby and severed my grandmother's leg just above the knee after a train literally rolled over her while trying to escape. My grandfather carried her and her severed leg five or six miles in the freezing weather to a veterinary clinic in the city. He broke in and found what he needed to stop the bleeding, cauterize her leg, and ultimately save her life.

The man had an amazing toughness and the ability to make things happen. He earned a PhD in Veterinarian Sciences and became a Professor at the University of Georgia, where he had started the first soccer and flying clubs on campus. From there, he had worked his way into the Pan American and World Health Organizations, traveling the world as a diplomat. He spoke fluently in at least thirteen languages.

He became a self-made, successful businessman. At one point, he owned over 100 acres in Athens where he developed over 150 rental apartments. It was his influence that inspired my love of real estate, appreciation for architecture, and entrepreneurial spirit.

However, the people closest to him also knew a different side of my grandfather, and I had heard enough from my mother to be wary about living with him. She knew him as a cold and selfish man who often misled others—including family members—for personal gain. When my mother was pregnant with me in 1965, she and my father needed a car. They scraped together enough money to buy a used Opel from my grandfather, who assured them it was a "deal." When it immediately broke down, she took it to the repair shop where her father regularly had it serviced. The mechanic let her know he had told her father the car was worthless. When Mom tearfully confronted her father with the truth, he wouldn't pay for the repair or buy back the car. Instead, he coldly proclaimed, "Take this as a lesson. If your own family can take advantage of you, what will the world do when given the chance?"

My grandfather's character hadn't improved since then. One time I told him he was unfair and unloving, and he used the heel of his heavy dress shoe to beat me while I was balled up on the ground, until my ear bled. He cheated on my grandmother until the day she finally divorced him at age sixty-seven.

In contrast, my grandmother was about as sweet as they come and good to the core, despite all the pain she had suffered in her life. In addition to the loss of her leg at nineteen and marriage to someone who turned out to be an insensitive and apathetic husband, she had lost her oldest son in his early twenties. She lived her life cooking, cleaning, and living on a paltry budget, wearing thrift-store clothes.

My grandmother was a consistently shining light while I was trying to endure the abuse of my grandfather. She was always sweet and loving even though she had no influence or voice over his demeanor. I was proud when she finally mustered the courage to divorce him. Although her final years proved a lonely time, they provided the peace and dignity she deserved.

After only a year and a half with my grandparents, I overheard my grandfather on the phone talking to my mother. He reminded her that I was her responsibility, so in 1981 I found myself on a flight to South America to live with mom and her third husband, Napoleon. He wasn't the best father figure I'd had so far, but he wasn't the worst, either. It probably didn't help that we didn't share a common language, mine English and his Spanish. He worked hard, with determination and purpose, and expected everyone around him to do the same. He could fix anything and wasn't afraid of long days spent with work-intensive projects. He was like my grandfather in that way and I always wondered if that was why my mother was attracted to him.

I was sixteen and living in an Andes village where the streets were often gravel and dirt, oxen roamed the fields, and I had to go outside and fill a bucket with water if I wanted to flush the toilet. It quickly became evident to me that I was imposing on a simple lifestyle that Mom and Napoleon had created for themselves.

Before long they had arranged for me to accompany a traveling Venezuelan missionary named Johnny. This decision was the opposite of what I had in mind, but something inside me said to accept the challenge, and frankly, I needed a break from my mom. I hadn't lived with her for many years, and years later I uncovered some deep wounds that were still raw from her departure from my life and the consequences of her decisions.

Johnny was an absolute stranger, and I was about to jump into a camper truck with him and head into the most dangerous parts of Venezuela! What could possibly go wrong? Oh, and one more twist in the story: he didn't speak a lick of English, and I only knew a couple of words in Spanish. Talk about a relational challenge! But we quickly taught each other a handful of critical terms like "Stop the car" and "Where's the nearest bathroom?" I learned more Spanish than he learned English, but from day one, I was committed to help him as we wandered from town to town in remote portions of Venezuela, often near the Colombian border. We slept in his camper truck or, if lucky, in the home of someone from a local village church willing to take us in. On occasional nights in the home of a generous supporter of the mission, sleeping in a hammock with a portable fan in the blazing heat was heavenly. I assumed it was like a night at the Ritz . . . which I could only imagine.

I learned a lot more than Spanish from Johnny. He had conviction and a servant's heart for the Lord. We shared many experiences along the Columbian border, several involving military checkpoints complete with machine guns and our (hopefully) convincing explanations of what we were doing there. We also met many poor families who lovingly opened their doors and generously shared their food and homes with us. Johnny and I not only survived our travels, but also became great friends.

But after six weeks on the road with this bizarre and inspiring road trip, I knew it was time to go home. I had God in my heart like never before, having witnessed real faith in Johnny's commitment to serve. I was beginning to realize my destiny was bigger than my circumstances, and that self-pity was not the path to success. This was a new feeling, and one I hadn't felt in quite some time. I was now confident and optimistic about life and its potential, and after seeing what poverty really looked like, I was also grateful and humble to the core.

I left Venezuela feeling fortunate for the experience and the personal growth I had experienced during my short time there. Feeling blessed replaced my prior feelings of resentment from being abandoned and neglected. I left hopeful and optimistic even in the face of many unknowns ahead.

By this time I was seventeen and a half, but I'd missed so much school from being passed from one family to another that I was two years behind. Now I needed a place to stay long enough to jump back into the middle of tenth grade and resume my path to graduation and beyond. My grandparents in Georgia allowed me stay with them again, but only for a couple of weeks while I called every relative, friend, and neighbor I could think of.

The first call was to my adoptive father and stepmother's home where I received a thoughtful but resounding "No." Their response was justified due to lots of family unrest and teens of their own living within a limited space.

My second call was to the man I had hoped would become my stepfather, but I discovered he was still in prison. So much for that option.

I even took a one-way bus ride to upstate New York to talk to my biological father. Not really knowing the dire nature of my situation (which I soft sold not to feel rejected if it went that way), he declined to take me in, citing a young family with little space for a nearly grown seventeen-year-old boy. After years of disconnect and zero communication, I can't blame him.

I'd given Venezuela a try, and Mom wasn't moving back to the U.S. . . . so scratch that possibility off the list. I felt like one of those old dogs at the pound, regularly passed over for younger and cuter puppies. But the evidence was clear: from now on, my life would be up to me. I had no one else to call or ask for favors. Out of options for now, yet armed with a positive belief that God had a plan for me, I returned to my grandparents' home in Athens to figure out what to do next.

On previous visits, my grandmother had taken me to a local Methodist church, so she suggested I meet with the pastor for possible suggestions. He suggested I visit a children's home for orphans in Atlanta, a place funded by his denomination. That was an option that would never have crossed my mind, but my grandmother drove me to Atlanta to check it out.

The home was in a sketchy-looking area of downtown, but a friendly and sympathetic woman helped me fill out some paperwork and set up an interview with the resident therapist, who gave me a battery of tests. Within a week, they called to tell me I had been approved.

Although the large rooms with rows of beds at the children's home reminded me of military school, this time I was mentally and emotionally prepared. For the first time in many years, I controlled my own destiny. This was a choice I was making on my own.

On the evening before I was scheduled to move in, I called my adoptive father and his wife to tell them my plans and invite them to visit me sometime. They thought that was a good idea and told me they were looking forward to spending time reconnecting after not seeing me for the past seven years. Then, not even fifteen minutes later, they called back, clearly in tears. They asked my forgiveness for not truly understanding the severity of my situation and offered to let me stay with them for the balance of high school. When they had originally declined my request to live with them after I returned from Venezuela, they assumed some other family member would take me in. They never dreamed my next best option would be a children's home.

I gladly accepted their apology . . . and their invitation. I never took their love for granted. My next two and a half years with them in Conyers, Georgia, were as normal as I had ever experienced. I engaged with them at home and began attending church where I officially accepted Christ and I did my best to be a role model for my siblings there. By the end of that time, I made a few lifelong friends, landed solid grades, and gained acceptance to Georgia State University and the University of Georgia. From that point, I began to be self-sufficient and take care of myself.

So, I assure you, I didn't have an easy life. It was turbulent at times and about as bumpy a road through childhood as you'll find. No consistent role models. No attentive parents who consistently showed me how to build a life of commitment, contribution, and creativity. No private school education. No trust funds as pathways to the best colleges.

I often felt hurt and abandoned, but now I can see why everyone made the choices they did at the time. Aristotle said that "choice and not chance determines your destiny," and I've chosen to love and forgive them all. As an adult, I have reconnected with most of them, and they have taught me some valuable lessons. I've found it far easier to forgive than to carry perpetual bitterness and resentment. I can attest to the fact that your past does not determine your future.

Any dark clouds I endured during my childhood came with the silver linings of important lessons learned—lessons about personal character, persistence, enduring hope, faith, and more. I emerged from my turbulent childhood stronger, wiser, and eager to face the adult world. I would soon discover a new awareness and sense of purpose, which would endure throughout my lifetime.

Sometimes, I don't check my GPS until I'm already stuck in a traffic jam. Some of us begin our adult years and careers metaphorically stuck in a ditch or on a confusing detour. I know what that's like because I was in the same condition. Even then, we can use our GPS—the input and feedback from people we trust—to find the best way forward. It's never too late (or too early) to craft a sound, workable, inspiring plan for the next year, the next five years, and the next fifty years.

At the end of each chapter, you'll find some questions. These are designed to help you reflect more specifically on your past, your present, and your future. They're also very helpful for team leaders (and friends) to stimulate discussion and application of the principles in the chapters. Take your time with these. You'll be glad you did . . . I guarantee it. I hope that each chapter will bring you one step closer to a life with no regrets.

QUESTIONS TO CONSIDER:

1. Why did you choose this book to read? What, specifically, are you hoping to learn from it?

2. What would need to happen for you to be able to say, five or even fifty years from today, "My life was awesome!"? What currently threatens to keep you from achieving that level of satisfaction?

3. Have you invested 10,000 hours into mastering any specific skill or ability? If not, what's the closest you have come? Do you think you need to focus more time and attention on one specific interest of yours? What might happen if you invested in yourself with that level of commitment?

4. How has your past impeded your success in the present? How can you resolve lingering problems from the past to secure a more successful future?

5. What are some silver linings you have discovered from the gloomy events of your past?

CHAPTER 2

A LIFE WITH PURPOSE

Pygmalion was a sculptor in Greek mythology. According to the Roman poet Ovid, he could look at a piece of marble and see the sculpture trapped inside it. Ovid also wrote that Pygmalion had become disgusted and disinterested in women after witnessing the shameful behavior of a cult of prostitutes. He committed himself to celibacy and began to carve his version of an ideal woman, whom he named Galatea, out of ivory.

Galatea was more than a statue to him. She represented every hope, every dream, every opportunity in life. Over time, Pygmalion fell in love with the possibility of his ideal coming to life. His unspoken desire was to have a living version of his creation. One day he kissed his statue and at that moment Galatea became quite real. (According to the myth, the goddess Aphrodite was at work.) This account has been retold in many various ways throughout the centuries. Perhaps the most well-known is the George Bernard Shaw play, *Pygmalion*, that spawned the Broadway musical *My Fair Lady*.

Why do you suppose this concept was so well-received? I think it's because most of us have some ideal we'd love to see become a reality. For Pygmalion, it was a physical relationship. For you, it might be securing a specific job, starting your own company, upgrading your self-image, or any number of things. But perhaps you're assuming the odds of that happening are about as good as an ivory statue springing to life if you wish hard enough.

I've discovered that people are often surprised (shocked, even) when they quit wishing and start planning to make that dream come true. Sometimes all it takes is a minor mental adjustment to create phenomenal change, as was demonstrated in what has been called "one of the most inspiring and widely cited breakthroughs in the history of psychology."

In 1964, Harvard psychologist Robert Rosenthal visited an elementary school in San Francisco with permission to give students there "the Harvard Test of Inflected Acquisition." He told the faculty that the test would indicate which children in each classroom were expected to "bloom" academically. Sure enough, a year later, the first-graders who had been designated had increased their IQ scores by an average of 27 points. That's when Rosenthal made a stunning confession: he had been lying. The fancy-sounding exam had been a standard IQ test, and the "bloomers" had been selected randomly. Many came from low-income Mexican families. Rosenthal's experiment had demonstrated that it was the teachers' belief in their pupils' potential, not any innate advantage, that spurred the students to achieve.

Rosenthal called the result of his experiment The Pygmalion Effect. In the decades since, it has become a classic lesson taught to education and psychology students, and has been applied to various settings requiring inspired leadership, including military units, business settings, family homes, and courtrooms.

"GOD HAS BIG PLANS FOR YOU"

If you'll indulge me, I want to share one more personal family story that I left out of the previous chapter. It was the first time I personally experienced the Pygmalion Effect.

When I was nine years old, I took my first trip out of the country to spend the summer with my grandparents and my mother, who were living in Caracas, Venezuela at the time. As I've mentioned, my grandmother only had one leg after a run-in with a train, but she was strong and resilient. My grandfather often took her to a remote area with hot springs because it soothed her arthritic muscles. The three of us had traveled for several hours to arrive at a mountain village near a large natural hot spring. After we unpacked, the two of them wanted to get some rest, so my grandfather handed me a couple of coins and suggested I go down to the springs and swim. I don't know exactly how a Venezuelan bolivar compared to a U.S. dollar, but I remember that one would buy me a grape soda and a bag of chips.

I took the money and headed down the dirt path towards the water. It was a different time then. I was often allowed to roam free with no one watching me, and I never thought anything of it. I felt freedom was a badge of honor, and I wore it proudly.

The pool was set against a mountain of trees buried deep in the rainforest, and it was a gorgeous sunny day. The sun was peeking out from behind the mountains, casting shadows on the ground around me as four young Venezuelan boys ran down toward the pool. They appeared to be friends, laughing and smiling as they sprinted toward the water. They were clearly locals who weren't staying in the hotel. Only a few other people were there, lounging by the pool, but no one was swimming.

As the boys reached the edge of the hot-spring-fed pool, all four jumped in excitedly. But only three came up from under the warm water. Where the fourth boy had jumped in, I simply heard gurgling noises and saw bubbles at the surface of the water. He popped up once for a brief second, choking, and went back down. Up and down again. More bubbles and struggles.

I saw something no one else did: this boy was clearly drowning.

I looked around for an adult to help him. One man finally saw what was happening and ran to the edge of the pool, but he just stood there, seemingly frozen in place. I heard a woman scream, but she didn't jump in either. I realized no adult was there to save the day.

So, without hesitation, I threw down my grape soda and chips, and sprinted toward the water. Of course, I had no training for this sort of rescue. As I swam toward the boy, intent on helping, I didn't know that drowning victims are often hysterical and that they can pull you down with them in desperation.

He tried . . . aggressively, in fact. I was only a modest-sized nine-year-old, so I was unable to overpower him. Without a clue how to save him, I quickly took the deepest breath I could, plunged under the surface of the water, put my arms around his thighs, and paddled as fast as I could. As soon as I grabbed him, he went into hyper-panic mode, clawing and kicking the heck out of me. He used every ounce of his strength trying to drag me underwater with him. But I just kept kicking toward the edge of the pool.

Eventually, after a significant struggle, we reached the pool's edge. With the help of the "frozen" man still at poolside, the boy finally released the clumps of my hair firmly in his grasp and began to pull himself onto the concrete, coughing up pool water. Thank goodness the man was there to help him out, because my energy had been fully depleted in the water.

I climbed out beside my new Venezuelan friend as we both caught our breath, and a small crowd gathered around us to see if we were okay. We were. That boy was alive. I looked at him with amazement, thinking, *I just saved your life, kid.*

As I excitedly ran back to my grandparents' cabana, I kept replaying the incident in my mind. It was surreal and almost felt like a dream. It was the kind of story every kid imagines in his head—like being called off the bench with two outs in the bottom of the ninth to hit a home run and win for your team, or sinking a last-second buzzer beater on the basketball court to pull ahead, or any number of other scenarios of being the hero at a crucial moment. Kids never expect those things to ever happen in real life, and now that it had for me, I didn't know how to respond.

I wondered if my grandparents would even believe me. When they heard my news, my grandfather was a bit dismissive and didn't make a big deal about it. But not my grandmother. She placed her hands on my face and, with tears in her eyes, said something that day that impacted my self-perspective and belief for life. She said, "You are a gift from God, Ricky. You were placed here today to save that boy's life, and God has big plans for you."

I believed her. And I never forgot it.

That was the second miracle of that day. A seed was planted in my life when my grandmother assured me that my life mattered and that I was a favored child of God. Even throughout the turmoil of my childhood, I continued to believe that my life had purpose, that I could accomplish something good, and maybe even change the world. Her words were, to me, the Pygmalion Effect on steroids.

WHAT ARE THE ODDS?

How do you think your world might change if you truly believed that *your* life had purpose—that you were on earth for a reason? If no one has ever told you this before, let me assure you: your life *does* have purpose. You'll need to learn to suspend personal insecurities and self-criticism before you can even begin to think in such terms. But after you do, you'll want to ask yourself, *Why can't I feel like this more often . . . loved, confident, and encouraged to dream?*

You may assume the odds of that happening are too high to waste your time thinking about. But if so, consider this: the very fact that you are alive on earth proves that you have already beaten phenomenally high odds. Don't take my word for it. During a TEDx Talk in 2011, author Mel Robbins mentioned that the odds of being born are one in 400 trillion. Her comment wasn't taken at face value by one of the people in her audience that day. Dr. Ali Binazir had degrees from Berkeley and Cambridge, and was working at Harvard. He did the math himself, calculating odds of your parents meeting, odds of their staying together long enough to have children, odds of everyone in your lineage (for the length of human existence) having lived long enough to have children, odds of just the right sperm connecting with just the right egg 150,000 times to produce your ancestors, right up to your parents producing you rather than a sibling.

All told, those odds add up to a one in 102,685,000 likelihood that you'd be reading this today. (That number is 10 followed by 2,685,000 zeroes.) Those odds are essentially a zero probability, and yet there you are.

So the question then becomes: Now that you've arrived here in a miraculous series of events, what are you going to do with your life? Personally, I don't see it as an option; it's my obligation to quit settling and start living life to the fullest.

Your life experiences are unique to you, like no one else's. You have a purpose to fulfill that no one else can do as well. I believe you beat the long odds and are here today for a reason. One of the first realizations we all need to make to live life to the fullest is a simple truth that should be obvious, yet many people seem to miss it: *There are lots of people on earth besides you.*

Don't you know people who attempt to live, whether intentionally or subconsciously, like they're the only people who matter? They try to insulate themselves from the world with bigger homes and estates, all the best food, and luxurious living at every level. Or if they don't have sufficient financial means, they simply withdraw into their own world, refusing to let anyone else in. Maybe you've tried one of those options yourself. If so, you probably found that such a lifestyle wasn't nearly as satisfying as you anticipated.

People around you are drowning. Do you see them? And if so, do you just stand there, frozen, waiting for someone else to act?

Saving a life can be as simple as offering a sincere smile at just the right time to someone who is discouraged. It can be showing love to someone feeling unlovable. Being freer with kind words and compliments is like throwing out lifejackets to people who just can't seem to get out from under the burdens of their lives that keep pulling them underwater.

None of the other steps to success that follow in this book will be as powerful if you aren't convinced that your life has purpose. If your driving goal is to accumulate all you can so you can live the most self-indulgent life possible, you will go down a much different path: You're headed for a midlife crisis at forty or fifty, or even worse, on your last day on Earth, you'll ask yourself, *Why didn't I do things differently?*

Start today with a foundational belief that your life has purpose. That's putting your ultimate destination into your GPS. If you don't know where you want to go, that's fine for the moment, but find out! Do the personal reflection to determine how you want your life to count. I'm not talking about titles or prestige or enormous wealth. Those things may come, but they're not what truly fulfills us. Find a mentor or life coach who will help you sort through your unique blend of talents, passions, experiences and opportunities . . . and don't stop until you have a purpose that burns in your heart and fills your mind with visions of how you can have an impact on others. Let me give you an example of someone who demonstrates this awareness better than I ever can.

When Aidan Anderson was a young boy, he and his mother didn't have much. They were on their own, but they felt a lot of gratitude for one another and they decided to do whatever they could to help others. It's the kind of thing lots of us do at Christmas, and perhaps another time or two during the year to make ourselves feel good, but Aidan and his mom made this a regular practice—everywhere and every day.

One day when Aidan was in a restaurant, waiting for his family to finish dinner, he pulled out his harmonica and played an impromptu jam session, after which he received $80 in tips. He was only seven at the time, but realized he already had everything he really needed, so he donated the $80 to sick children in Africa. According to his website, "That one simple choice to give changed his life and put him on his path of purpose."

Aidan's persistent desire to help those in need soon led to new and bigger opportunities, including regular support for kids with pediatric cancer. He began to be featured in many forums, including TEDx Talks and on the *Today Show*. He now works through his own organization, Aidan Cares. At the age of sixteen, Aidan has traveled the world and inspired millions, all from a simple belief that his life is designed to help others.

ASKING THE RIGHT QUESTIONS

But don't miss the significance that Aidan's influence started small, at a local level. For instance, if he and his mom were walking into a grocery store, they would stop and look for evidence of a need. They would scan the parking lot, asking one another, "Who might be hurting here? How can we encourage them?"

Aiden is still volunteering and sharing his kindness. In a recent speech, he said that he felt that "generations are dying inside because they aren't living out their passions." Is that you? If it is, to what extent? What if you had real focus and clarity, coupled with resources to elevate all areas of life and make a difference? What would that look and feel like? Where might your time, influence, and capital make the most difference?

This questioning approach is effective because the subconscious brain is powerful and never stops working to solve riddles . . . riddles you pose through your thoughts and experiences. If you ask yourself, "Who can I serve?" your eyes will suddenly be opened and you will begin to see those you can help. If you ask, "How can I make a difference right here where I am?" you will find the answer.

Within your brain is something called the reticular activating system (RAS)—a collection of cells located throughout the brainstem that affect, among other things, your attention, arousal, and ability to focus. Reticular activation consciously triggers your brain to look for and notice specific things in your environment. The science involved is a bit complex, but here is a simple way to understand the concept.

Let's say you see a magazine ad and decide you might like to buy a Range Rover, even though you'd never really noticed that model of vehicle before. But then, lo and behold, you start seeing Range Rovers everywhere. You pass several on the way to work the next morning. You see a couple in the parking lot. You notice television ads promoting Range Rovers. Suddenly, they're everywhere!

Did more Range Rovers suddenly fill the streets? Is it a coincidence?

No. Your RAS has alerted your subconscious mind that you have an interest in Range Rovers, and your subconscious mind is working on your behalf all the time, even when you are asleep. With a little practice, you can learn to make your reticular activating system work for you. As Napoleon Hill has noted: "Whatever the mind can conceive and believe, it can *achieve.*"

One technique that I have used for years is starting every morning by thinking, *Today is going to be an awesome, amazing day. I can't wait to meet cool, unique, and powerful people and look for ways to add value to everyone I meet.* That is a short-term method for using reticular activation. In the long-term, this technique can activate your brain to streamline your five-year, ten-year, and twenty-year vision.

Here are some questions that can activate your brain in positive ways:

- What would I do if I knew I couldn't fail?
- How does God (or your higher power) want to use me today?
- Who can I help in my neighborhood, job, church, and school?
- What are generous, committed people accomplishing in my city and how can I become a part of it?
- How can I make a difference today?

Of course, just as your reticular activating system can work to your benefit, it can also be detrimental to your emotional health and mindset if you aren't careful. Here are some questions that keep your mind running in circles, accomplishing nothing but frustration:

- What's wrong with me?
- Why do I always seem to fail, no matter what I attempt?
- Why bother trying so hard?
- What is the point anyway?

These questions also activate your brain, but they drain your energy. Remember, your brain wants to solve riddles. It works just as hard trying to answer "Why am I such a loser?" as it does to determine "How can I help the most people in the best way?"

Tony Robbins says, "Successful people ask better questions, and as a result, they get better answers." That's why affirmations and positive influences are so powerful. You think it, and your brain tries to solve it even when you're not conscious it's doing so.

Here's one question I suggest you ask yourself regularly: "How can I focus so intentionally on my gifts and talents that my weaknesses become irrelevant?" When you answer that, you'll find real joy in your work and personal life. It requires far less energy to develop your strengths than to attempt to overcome your weaknesses. You simply don't have to be good at everything. Look around. Who is?

Start asking the right questions. Those answers will lead to your greatest self, while asking the wrong questions only hold you back.

FIRST AND LAST

I think it's vital to be honest with yourself, but that doesn't mean you can't be positive. In order to keep my brain primed for positive answers and perspective, I have a habit called "First and Last." I intentionally try to be aware of my thoughts first thing in the morning and last thing at night.

I no longer wake up and check my email right away. I don't allow my thoughts to be hijacked the moment I awaken. Instead, I have established a routine to establish a good mental state as I start my day.

First, I go to a physical space that inspires me. We live in a house with a second-floor wall of windows, overlooking the most magnificent trees and panoramic views of nature. This is my happy place, so I often start my day there. Most days, the light of the sun fills the room first thing in the morning, infusing me with energy and a sense of aliveness. It's almost impossible to think negative thoughts in this place.

Once there, I begin thinking of what I'm truly grateful for. I go through my mental rolodex of people, recent lessons learned, and unexpected fortunate events I consider gifts of grace, feeling truly thankful for each item that comes to mind. I have found that when I start with gratitude, I become more grounded, focused, and aware of how good life can be.

Next, I channel my thoughts to the people I'm meeting that day and how I can bring positive energy to them. I focus on how to contribute the most value and end up with the best possible results. Even when I expect conflict, I try to envision a positive outcome.

I often use a prayer I learned from Andy Stanley: "Lord, give me the wisdom to know what is best and the courage to act on it." I follow that morning prayer with a simple reminder that someone's going to accomplish great things today, so why not me? I also want to start the day thanking God for all the good things He has given me, and asking Him for wisdom to do good that day. It keeps me on track for a life with purpose.

(Please be clear that I'm explaining what works for me. I realize people have different faiths and different higher powers than I do. Yet regardless of one's faith, I believe that if we remain attentive, the spiritual world shows up in many ways. I encourage you to stay open to the miraculous moments in your life that draw you toward a higher power. It's part of the contemplative journey that creates a richer and fuller life.)

After my quiet time, I finally glance at my texts, though I am just checking for 9-1-1 emergencies. If someone sends me a text at 6:30 or

7:00 A.M., it's probably important. I still rarely check my email at this point, though.

Next, I head to the shower where I try to remain in the same state of prayer and gratitude. I often kneel in the shower and simply humble myself before God in complete surrender. Something about this state of complete vulnerability feeds my soul and reminds me that God is the giver of life and of everything I have. I like the observation of Pierre Teilhard de Chardin, a French philosopher, paleontologist, and Jesuit priest: "We are not human beings having a spiritual experience. We are spiritual beings having a human experience."

I've also learned that if I take about forty deep, controlled breaths, it helps me establish a more positive and productive mindset. There's a scientific reason to explain why, but I just know it works for me in the morning and anytime I feel tension creeping in throughout the day when I'm beset by challenges and projects.

If time allows, some mornings I pick up an electric guitar (unplugged so I don't wake the house up early) and strum a few chords. I like to physically feel the positive vibrations. I continue to ask myself, *What am I grateful for?* and *Who can I serve today, and how?* I've found that most grateful people are pretty darn happy and have an extraordinary capacity to cope with negative situations.

Of course, even though you might try to start every morning with a positive and uplifting mindset, not every moment will be perfect. Some days will be downright awful. Many days while I was suffering through a painful divorce beyond my control, I would just kneel in the shower with my face to the ground, literally touching the cool tile. Yet eventually I learned to see that although my temporary pain had blinded me to the beautiful aspects of life, those things hadn't disappeared. I began to redirect my focus from my misery to acknowledge the good things I *hadn't* lost. I even slowly regained my sense of humor (although admittedly it was dark humor at first). But I can assure you that a capacity to confront your personal pain while applying humor is a real gift to yourself.

One of the first things I was taught at Keller Williams was that if you change the way you look at things, the things you look at change. Give it a try; it's a powerful antidote to disappointment and despair. You control your thoughts and decide what dwells in your mind over time. When you focus on the good, there's less room for the bad to take root and remain in your heart and mind. Grateful and resentful just can't live in the same space. You can reframe any circumstance any time simply by choosing to expand your perspective.

If you want additional ideas or inspiration, I highly recommend Hal Elrod's book, *The Miracle Morning: The 6 Habits That Will Transform Your Life before 8 AM*. He uses the acronym SAVERS to remind readers of the importance of Silence, Affirmations, Visualization, Exercise, Reading, and Scribing (writing/journaling). Success lies in your habits, and so does mediocrity and failure. I've always dreaded the idea of a 6 a.m. workout, but I've never regretted one! And they only happen when they're part of an established, accountability-based habit. That goes for all of the SAVERS strategies for a rocket-launched, balanced day. Read Hal's book, put it into action, and I assure you your days will start off powerfully and purposefully!

After a long day, I try to refocus my thoughts on positive things again before I go to bed. Why fall asleep worrying about things you can't control, or dreading the day to come? If you're about to turn your brain over to your subconscious for six to eight hours, why not point it in the right direction? Give it an uplifting riddle to solve or narrative to enjoy.

For me, after family time in the evening, I find the last few minutes right before falling asleep to be ideal for a devotional, an upbeat podcast, or any content that inspires quality thinking. I also find it to be a perfect time to reflect on my day and the positive experiences I had with people. If you've never attempted a regimen of deep thinking or a regular focus on spiritual purpose and gratitude, this is a great place to start and great for rebalancing your energy. And then looking forward, begin to ponder worthwhile questions, such as "How can I engage in a positive way that leaves the world a better place?" You may not arrive at any satisfactory answers right away, but keep asking great questions and trust that you'll eventually achieve some meaningful insight.

Try starting and ending each day with the confidence that you're here for a reason, your life counts, and the world has good work for you to do. And even with negative experiences in circumstances and with people, practice forgiveness (toward yourself and others) and learn valuable lessons so the experience wasn't wasted. Done regularly, it will prime your brain and your subconscious to reveal ways to serve and fulfill your personal mission on earth. That's truly seeking and living into your best life—a life of purpose, without regrets. I'm far from perfect in this practice, but even a few times a week can make a lot of difference in the version of me that shows up at home and at work.

CHOOSING THE BEST

Everyone has the opportunity to do (or at least try) what I'm suggesting, but not everyone will. Many just aren't that committed to start with. Others will give it a half-hearted attempt, but quickly find an excuse to return to the comfortable pace of mediocrity. Lots of people will encounter a bit of challenge or difficulty, and then immediately begin to complain that their life just isn't as good or secure as other people's lives. These are all ways we choose defeat and failure rather than growth and success. People who stick it out, however, have learned it's the difficulties they face and overcome that make them stronger.

This blend of tenacity and understanding will allow you to be more patient with yourself and take bold steps toward the best version of yourself.

**DO SOMETHING HARD EVERY DAY,
AND YOU'LL HAVE MORE CONFIDENCE IN
EVERYTHING YOU DO.**

Muscles grow stronger when we exert them so much that we feel weak. In the same way, passion, determination, and skills grow stronger when they're tested to their limits. We may think we want an easy, carefree life, but it appears that the vast majority of people who live that way are bored to death! Challenges are the stairs to greatness, and tenacity is an essential quality for those who want to make a difference. Here are a few comments from people who have tested their limits:

Angela Lee Duckworth: "Grit is sticking with your future day in, day out and not just for the week, not just for the month, but for years."

T.S. Eliot: "Only those who will risk going too far can possibly find out how far one can go."

Michael Jordan: "If you quit once it becomes a habit. Never quit!"

John Ortberg: "Over time, grit is what separates fruitful lives from aimlessness."

Thomas Edison: "Many of life's failures are people who did not realize how close they were to success when they gave up."

James Michener: "Character consists of what you do on the third and fourth tries."

Amelia Earhart: "The most difficult thing is the decision to act. The rest is merely tenacity. The fears are paper tigers. You can do anything you decide to do. You can act to change and control your life and the procedure. The process is its own reward."

George Clooney: "The best lesson my mom taught me was how to be scrappy."

Sometimes, challenges come out of nowhere, but we can also push ourselves into situations that require us to summon all our courage and skills to succeed. Either way, when you look back at your accomplishment, you can say, "I did it!" And if feels so good. Since facing difficulties is such a productive exercise, why not make it part of your daily practice? You'll find that the natural tendency to cut corners, exaggerate, and minimize requires us to develop that most important character quality: integrity, which is "the quality of being honest and having strong moral principles." I like the second definition, too: "the state of being whole and undivided." When our minds and hearts are divided, we waver between the important and the expedient, the honorable and the selfish. A "whole" heart happens when our outside behavior aligns with our inside voice. When we drift toward expedience and selfishness, we try to validate our decisions and justify our actions. Sooner or later, we may even believe the lies we tell ourselves. It's wise to notice and navigate the very human temptation to drift, and it's healthy to forgive and seek forgiveness when we've given in to that temptation. No matter who you are and what you've done, there's an opportunity to start over. Take it. You won't regret it.

The writer who has perhaps been the most influential in persuading me to choose wisely is Viktor Frankl. He knew real struggle and the emotional pain of hopelessness while laboring in four concentration camps, including Auschwitz, during World War II. He lost his parents, his brother, and his pregnant wife. Yet amid all the horror and pain, he reached an amazing conclusion: "Everything can be taken from a man but one thing: the last of the human freedoms—to choose one's attitude in any given set of circumstances, to choose one's own way." Viktor Frankl was one of those rare individuals who refused to allow *anything* to destroy his hope or cause him to settle for less than the best he could achieve.

Sean Stephenson was another. Born with a rare bone disorder that stunted his growth, he wasn't expected to survive. Although confined to a wheelchair for life, he earned a doctorate and became a board-certified therapist, international speaker, and best-selling author. His book, *Get Off Your "But,"* is empowering!

Sadly, Sean recently passed away unexpectedly, only months after I met him. But what I know is that he chose to live on his terms. He had very few easy days, if any, but chose a life of engaged purpose. And on his last day, he felt at peace because despite the many challenges during his journey, he battled to become the man his Creator intended. In Sean's TEDx talk, "Infinite Possibilities: TEDx Ironwood State Prison," he tells inmates, "Never believe a prediction that does not empower you." For inmates and the rest of us, it's smart to ask ourselves, "Whose voice am I listening to? What impact is it having on me? What voice do I need to hear . . . and hear right now?"

You can choose to be more persistent, more intentional about your influence on others, and more conscientious about making your life count. Or you can choose to settle for less. My life changed from the moment my grandmother placed her hands on my face, looked me in the eye, and said, "Your life has purpose. You are going to help so many people." Do *you* need someone to remind you that you're special and have unrealized capacity that, if unlocked, changes everything?

If you've never had anyone affirm you in that way, I'm doing it now. You will experience much more joy and contentment if you first believe you're here for a purpose. Can you accept that as a fact? Forget about whatever has been holding you back and making you feel unsure of yourself. Take deep breaths and tell yourself repeatedly this week: "My life has purpose. I am going to become my best, achieve at a high level, and make a difference along the way."

If you need professional help to work through old experiences and wounds, no shame in that. We all need help sometimes to rescript the lingering hurtful memories of our past. Even if your past is something you're not proud of, forgive yourself for what has happened (or perhaps what hasn't happened). Just admit your past failures and shortcomings, and then change the trajectory of your life. In time, you'll see that your wounds and flaws are what make you special and relatable. They make you a far greater source of inspiration and connectivity to the world around you.

You are here for a reason. You've beaten the odds to be here. You have a dream you'd like to see come to life and a purpose to fulfill. Let's turn our attention now to some specific ways to help you do that.

QUESTIONS TO CONSIDER:

1. Have you ever personally experienced the Pygmalion Effect where someone saw something good in you that no one else saw and helped you become more confident and self-assured?

    If so, have you begun to do the same for others?

2. Have you ever tried to identify your purpose? If so, what is it? If not, begin to give the matter serious thought. (Don't be shy about asking trusted friends for their input regarding your talents, strengths, and abilities.)

3. How would your life be different if you had a firmer belief that you matter immensely to your family, community, and world?

4. Who are some people who have inspired (or might inspire) you to be your best? What steps do you need to take to begin to live up to that expectation?

5. What questions are you asking yourself? Are you activating your mind to solve puzzles that will have a positive result, or do your mental questions reinforce negativity?

6. Do you have a daily time set aside to tune out the world, assess the day, be positive, and express gratitude? If not, when can you start?

CHAPTER 3

LOOK FARTHER, THINK BIGGER

Many of life's most important lessons are learned during childhood, when we're not even trying to learn anything. It's funny, though, how many of them involve great disappointment.

I remember the day when Mr. Skipper, my fourth-grade band teacher, had us all line up to ask us our instrument of choice. I had heard that most of the girls would choose the flute or clarinet, and the guys usually ended up playing trumpet or some other brass instrument. But for those of us who wanted to be cool and lead the band, the most coveted choice was undisputedly the drums. I was a drummer at heart and I was ready to stake my claim.

When I got to the front of the line, I stepped right up to Mr. Skipper and proudly proclaimed, "Drums, sir!"

He took one look at me, grabbed my face, squeezed my cheeks, and forced my genetically gifted fat lips to make a kissy fish face. Then he spoke the most devastating words I could have imagined: "With those lips, young man, you are a trombone player." I was mortified and heartbroken. Dream crushed. Life over. Okay, I was getting a little melodramatic, but it certainly felt that way in that moment.

As it turned out, Mr. Skipper was right. I excelled at trombone. In ninth grade I played for the acclaimed Cedar Shoals High School marching band from Athens, Georgia. That year we marched in two premier half-time shows where I felt the energy of performance at an entirely different level. The first was in front of 50,000 spectators when the Atlanta Falcons played the L.A. Rams, and I thought that would be the highlight of my high school band experience. But then, a couple of weeks later, we played at the season opener between the University of Tennessee Volunteers and the Bulldogs of the University of Georgia. At the time, the 82,000 people in the stands were the largest crowd to ever watch the Dawgs play. What a thrill!

Even better, I learned that even if one dream got shattered and didn't work out for me, it was no reason to give up. I threw my energy and effort into a different pursuit and was rewarded with opportunities that few kids at that age ever achieve.

As it turned out, my plunge into fourth-grade trombone lessons began a lifelong love of playing music. During my first year of college I was taking a full load and working to pay for it, but leaving behind marching band had left me with more than a desire to play—I *needed* to make music. Not surprisingly, I couldn't find much demand for a solo trombonist, but I met a guy at work who was in a band that needed a bass player. Granted, a bass guitar is a far cry from a trombone, but I thought, *That sucker only has four strings, and you only play one note at a time for the most part. How hard could it be?*

THE GLORY DAYS OF SPIT BLUE AND OTHER MUSIC LESSONS

It didn't take me long to discover that playing bass isn't necessarily easier than six-string guitar, because great bass players are worth their weight in gold! It's up to the bass player, along with the drummer, to create the groove that supplies the energy and underbelly of a great song. I threw myself into learning my new instrument because I loved to create unique basslines for my newfound band.

The lead singer and primary songwriter was named Bill. I was eager to learn a few covers from other successful bands, but to Bill's credit, he saw sufficient talent and the requisite creativity in me and instead suggested our band write and perform our own music. I was nervous at first, but quickly realized that it was easier to write my *own* basslines than learn someone else's. (If it's your own creation, who can determine whether you're playing it right or wrong?) Besides, music is in the ear of the beholder.

The creative license I felt was a runway to full-on joy! We wrote good songs that didn't expose my lack of experience, and any of our minor shortcomings were amply compensated by the collaborative energy we produced when we played. It was just Bill, me, and a very capable drummer named Jeff, but we produced a surprisingly mature sound for a young three-piece band. We called ourselves Spit Blue. If you've even had a frozen blue Icee or slushy from a local convenience store, perhaps you can figure out why.

I regret to inform you that as much as we enjoyed playing together, Spit Blue never even made it to one-hit-wonder status. We disbanded and went our separate ways. But I was hooked on the joy of creating those tones and soundwaves driven by the electricity at my fingertips. I practiced fastidiously, and within three months was writing again with a new Atlanta band called Crave. We had a creative run of almost nine years and released two self-produced albums. We never made it to a level of rock stardom, but we did enjoy local success with a song in rotation on a college radio station in Atlanta. Consequently, we got some good write-ups, played local gigs about as often as we wanted, and got to rub shoulders with some very talented 90s bands in the pop and garage-rock genres.

No world tour, no big-label record deals, and no crowds anywhere close to 82,000 people—just lots of memories with good friends making good music that still make me smile. My fellow band members remain my friends to this day (more than twenty-five years later), and I still jam and share the stage with them periodically. They are two amazingly talented guys with heart and passion for music, a.k.a. my brothers from another mother, Stephen Brink and Steve Wiley! We were fronted by two different lead singers also committed to the journey, Simerly Cook and Suzanne Green. After that, I rocked out with Wiley, Adam Coletta, and Tall Paul (He's at least seven feet tall and makes me look very short on stage!) in a band we affectionately called Trainwreck, followed by a decade with a rock band with a country bent, The Dammages. Sean, Tammy, Jimmy and Brink are amazingly talented and have become an extension of my family. My current project is called Pushback, which includes some legends of rock: Jeff Chandler, Brink, Wiley, and Scott Hardy. A few additional folks I appreciate and have written music and played with are Francisco Vidal, The Bielenbergs, David Duncan, Bill Browder, Jeff from Spit Blue (my first band), and Bill Sawyer, drummer and friend who convinced me to borrow $500 from Franklin Financial to buy my first bass guitar while I was flat broke in college. As I recall, they loaned it to me at the bargain basement rate of 19% interest. I wisely paid it off quickly and poured my heart and soul into learning how to rock out and write music!

I've learned a lot about music theory and techniques from the various people I've played with. But more importantly, I've learned a life lesson that transcends music: when I associate with people who are better at something than I am, I will soon get better at it. I try as hard as anyone to be the best musician I can be, but I only get so far on my own. It's when I work with really gifted guitarists, bass players, drummers, and singers that I see marked improvement in my abilities.

This is the power of a role model. I don't believe that I've ever invented *anything*, but then, success doesn't require you to. Tony Robbins says, "Success leaves clues." He recommends you find someone who is succeeding at something you want to do and use his or her example as a model. This is the ultimate shortcut to success in all areas of life: learn from the best and then make it even better by applying what you learn to your own business or situation.

THE IMPORTANCE OF MENTORS

I remember scouting around during my first year in real estate sales to see who was killing it. Then I stared in the mirror and asked myself, *Do I have the capacity to replicate what they are doing?* I decided to use their standard as my new standard. I knew I could outwork most realtors competing for business, and that alone gave me a fantastic edge. Frankly, work ethic and tenacity may be the most underrated attributes of today's workforce. Most people fail to give 100 percent effort to anything, at least, not for very long.

In a moment of clarity, I also realized that I could choose an agent making $50,000 a year as my model . . . or I could emulate someone making $500,000. In real estate, the numbers don't lie. The failure rate for new agents is very high. Roughly eighty percent of first-time agents simply quit before the magic happens. I wanted to learn from those who had made it—more specifically, those who made it *big*. I planned to learn their ideas and their tricks, but then create something completely new by adapting those procedures to my perspective and personality.

I was greatly encouraged to discover that in real estate, sixty-eight percent of all clients go with the first realtor they find who appears to be capable. Wow! I didn't have to start out being the best; I just needed to get to the clients first and not blow it! Of course, as time went on, my skills improved and I got better. I still tried to outwork everyone else, but I also started out-networking and out-accommodating other agents.

For example, I noticed that great realtors always did something extra to deliver more than the client expected. There's even a Southern word for it that I learned from Kay Evans, the regional director and cofounder of Keller Williams Realty's southeast region: *lagniappe* [pronounced lan-*yap*, for you Northerners]. The French-derived word means "one extra," or a little unexpected bonus. It's often used in the food and pastry industry, like when you order a dozen pastries and you are delighted to discover the baker has thrown in "one extra" for free. Kay and her partner, Bob Kilinski, were both early mentors and role models to me, and they taught me about lagniappe in our business. Realtors who were earning six figures or more always operate well above the standard and then added a little something extra in a transaction that the client didn't expect.

I began to make it my goal that, even if my clients were already thrilled with our negotiation, I would throw in a last-minute surprise to add more value than they expected. I wanted them to know that I would go the extra mile to make them happy—that I was not just trying to make another sale.

Although I learned this by modeling great realtors around me, the way it played out in my business was completely different from theirs. Just by emulating those around me, I earned six figures during my first full year in real estate. By my fourth year, I was earning more than most executives, exceeding $300,000 in gross income. I am certain this would not have been possible if I was trying to figure everything out on my own. My mentors provided plenty of "satellite information" for my personal GPS, and I've found a good route from all the options.

Jon Shapiro was a mentor who encouraged me to hire an assistant my first year. I had only been a realtor for three months, and I first thought it was a ridiculous suggestion, particularly in 1996 and before closing my first transaction! But Jon was earning close to half a million a year, and I knew if I modeled a half-million-dollar guy, I could join him at the top.

I did whatever Jon suggested. I even cut my musician's rock-star trademark hair, which had grown comfortably to my shoulders. He also suggested selling my sport utility vehicle, bought new only a few months earlier, in favor of a luxury sedan. He told me, "Rick, you can't afford to lose even one client who judges you incorrectly. All walks of life, all ages and backgrounds need to find you appealing."

I trusted mentors who knew more than I did, with a successful track record to prove it, and that made all the difference. I have always heard that experience is a great teacher, even when it is not our own, and that you can skip a few steps on the ladder to success by starting on the rung where your mentor is standing.

Venturing out into a new career on your own is like trying to prepare a big meal by going into a kitchen filled with ingredients, but no recipes. Why spend your time in endless trial and error when there are so many cookbooks available from experienced gourmet chefs?

Whatever career you are pursuing, you can find abundant information from the experts if you'll take the time to look. Read their books and blogs. Listen to their podcasts. Attend their seminars. And when the opportunity presents itself, introduce yourself and see what advice those experts can offer to your specific situation. If they see you've done your research and are asking relevant questions, you might be able to have a conversation over a cup of coffee or maybe even buy them lunch. Be bold and creative, and do whatever it takes to learn from the best.

A SMALL FISH IN A BIG POND

In 2001, I was invited to Austin, along with twenty-five others, for a mastermind session with Gary Keller himself, founder and owner of

Keller Williams Realty. I had been in real estate for a little over five years and I was on pace to sell seventy-five houses with a reachable goal of earning $450,000 in commission. I thought I had made it, at least by peer standards and my dreams as a kid. At the request of Gary, he asked everyone to bring their best ideas to share with the group. I boarded the plane to Texas and started jotting down some notes, envisioning how my insights could help and encourage the other agents. I wanted to give back—to mentor those in the group like Jon had mentored me.

After my early and rapid success in real estate, I felt like a reasonably big fish who could add value to our meeting. But when I sat down in the group, I quickly realized I was the guppy in this pond. The agent to my right had a goal of $1.6 million that year. To his right was an agent on pace to reach two million dollars. Let me be clear: not two million in home sales volume, but a *commission* income of two million dollars in one year! I knew very few people at that point in my life netting a million dollars . . . certainly not two million.

What really astounded me, though, is that they were reaching those numbers with far fewer signs of the stress I was feeling (and, I'm sure, showing). To be honest, at that point in my career, I was already reaching a point of burnout. I worked with a team of two, but I was still regularly taking clients' calls late into the evening and even at night, and I was up before daylight in pursuit of success. Some days I felt like I was juggling chainsaws and losing body parts, but I assumed this pace was normal. I prided myself on being the guy they could call in a crisis. I told them, "If you're worried about the transaction and you need someone to talk you off a ledge any time, day or night, keep my number close." So they did.

My colleagues teased me of having CBT disease (I actually made up the term): Chronic Beeper Thigh. Remember beepers? I had one that aggressively vibrated so often with incoming messages that I began to anticipate it going off even when it wasn't. It was like I had a neurological disorder! I also had a cellphone (flip, of course) to stay connected with an answering service for "emergency calls"—which, of course, most became. (If you're young, you may not know that the first cellphones were very expensive and the companies charged by the minute, and an alpha-numeric pager was a device used to screen calls to see if the problem could wait until I could get back to the office and make a free call.)

I had developed a system that couldn't grow beyond our current number of clients. So as I sat amid that mastermind group of men and women who were doing double and triple my amount of sales while still enjoying lively and happy personal lives, I leaned in. I threw out my prepared notes and just listened.

After I recovered from the sudden deflation of my ego, I made some of the most amazingly successful friends and mentors in our company. We didn't know it at the time, but Gary Keller was using our group and a few others like it as research for a book he was working on: *The Millionaire Real Estate Agent*. It turned out to be one of the greatest books ever written for our industry, outlining the path to a million dollars in revenue. It's as relevant now as it was the day it was written and published, now approaching two decades ago.

I used Gary's book to build my million-dollar team, but over the years I've also used it to consult other business owners *not* in the real estate industry. The content transcends all industries with wisdom anyone can benefit from. In fact, roughly a third of the book focuses on mindset, the balance on systems, models, and strategies for success in business and life. It's been my foundation for years and I was honored to be among Gary's early masterminds who helped shape the content— and one another's careers—in significant ways.

**AND REMEMBER, IF YOU'RE THE SMARTEST PERSON
OR WEALTHIEST PERSON IN THE ROOM,
YOU'RE IN THE WRONG ROOM!**

That room with Gary Keller was absolutely the best room for me and my career in that season of life, and it was a gift to learn from the wisest and most experienced professionals in my industry. And now with the advent of COVID-19 inspired virtual training with Zoom, our company has access to his wisdom as well as that of many other leaders, like never before. That's clearly one huge silver lining created by the work-at-home culture we were forced to embrace for an unexpected season.

As I flew back home pondering all I had learned, my entire perspective shifted. My limiting beliefs about what was even possible had been blown out of the water. My sense of potential was now on a new level.

THE ROGER BANNISTER PRINCIPLE

Roger Bannister was the first man to run a mile in under four minutes. In the 1950s, most sports and medical experts agreed that this was an impossible feat. The previous record of 4:01:03 (four minutes, 1.3 seconds) had been held for nine years, and physiologists had warned Bannister that repeated attempts to break it would be dangerous to his health. If it ever happened, the experts said, it would have to be under ideal conditions: no wind, a temperature of sixty-eight degrees, on a hard, dry, clay track, and before a huge crowd cheering the runner on. Bannister's race took place on May 6, 1954, on a cold day and a wet track at a small meet at Oxford University. He finished the mile race with a time of 3:59:04, but the people present that day didn't learn the official time until later. As soon as the announcer on the loudspeaker spoke the word "three," the roar that rose from the jubilant crowd drowned out everything else.

All the naysayers of the past century were quieted in a single day. But the fascinating part of Bannister's record run is what happened next. Only forty-six days later, John Landy of Australia also broke the four-minute barrier. Just a year later, three runners *in the same race* did the same. And since then, more than a thousand runners have accomplished that "impossible" feat. In fact, the current record for the mile has dropped to 3:43:13.

Why did so many athletes suddenly begin to do what none had been able to do for centuries? It is because Roger Bannister broke their limiting belief. They no longer believed it to be impossible.

One athlete relates Bannister's success to that reticular activating system (RAS) I described in the previous chapter. I like how he applies the RAS to sports and competition:

> I love this [Roger Bannister] story. . . . When you become certain of something, when every part of your makeup believes it because you focus on it every single day, something "magical" happens. Not New Age magical, but science magical. We have a system in our bodies called the reticular activating system (RAS) that helps our brains decide what information to focus on and what to delete.

> When you have a clearly defined purpose, a mission, and when you live every moment in a state of certainty that you'll achieve it, you influence what your RAS filters out and what lights it up. As a result, you pay special attention [to] things that help you achieve what you're after, things you otherwise would have never noticed.

My reflection on all I had learned during my time with the mastermind group in Austin was my Roger Bannister moment. I began to envision a scenario where I could earn more and contribute more . . . and actually relish the process. I met people who were succeeding at the highest levels while still enjoying their personal lives. Before my opportunity to mingle with that group of super-achievers, my mind couldn't conceive of a scenario where I was this effective in business and this happy with life.

One of my greatest discoveries was an inverse relationship between the stress levels of a mega agent (a super high producer with a large and talented team) and that of a mid-level "do it all myself" producer. Creating next-level business meant more money to employ a bigger, more specialized staff team, and it increased my ability to stay focused on my one thing, my core genius, with freedom from any fear the details of the back office weren't getting done without my involvement. More production equals a far better life on many levels!

Some time ago, my son Luke had a Roger Bannister moment of his own. Luke was seventeen, on his high school track team, and specializing in the high jump. To stay in optimum shape, he treated his body like a temple. He ate well and trained hard, and he inspired me every day with his commitment to success for his team. Prior to his junior year, he had gradually increased the heights he could clear, but he seemed to have peaked at six feet. It looked like he had hit his threshold. Maybe six feet was the highest his body could jump. But then, during a competition in the spring of his junior year, Luke cleared six feet and two inches to establish a new personal best. On the way home, he told me, "Dad, I can no longer accept anything under six feet two inches."

Once he experienced what it was like to exceed what he thought he was capable of, he stopped thinking in terms of limits. He had broken one psychological barrier, and now he knew he could do it again. He could see it, feel it, and believe it. By the end of his junior season he had cleared six feet and four inches—more than his personal height of just under 6'2".

BOLDER THINKING, LONGER JUMPS

When I was thirty-five, my friend Jimmy Vaughn and I decided to buy dirt bikes at the same time—not just dirt bikes, but true motocross racing bikes. I didn't think thirty-five was too old to take up motocross racing . . . until I found myself beside Jimmy on our bikes on a local motocross racetrack. I'd love to tell you we were undaunted as we watched the racetrack regulars going approximately the speed of light and flying through the air over jumps ranging from a couple of feet to almost eighty feet. The truth is, we were mostly terrified. I remember wishing someone had suggested, "You know, you might want to learn to ride that high-powered motorcycle out in a field before you start making jumps on a track," but in our rush to glory, we hadn't thought that far ahead.

The first lap was humbling. I fell twice, and when I tried to jump a mere four-foot span, the motorcycle sprang to life with such ferocity it shot out from between my legs, leaving me on my ass. Thankfully my rear end wasn't as bruised as my ego.

Jimmy hadn't fared much better. As we met up to share our collective series of failed attempts, we noticed one fellow flying around the track like a winged gazelle. I kid you not—it was like magic how fast and smoothly he rode. Completely humbled and bewildered, we confessed our need for help and decided to ask him to share a few pointers. When he stopped for a break, I rode up beside him and tried to be casual. "Dude, you're really talented. . . . How does someone learn to ride and jump like that?"

He shrugged and said, "Just follow me. I'll pull you over the jumps!" [Okay, side note and reminder: one of the jumps was easily eighty feet long with ten-foot takeoff and landing ramps. You couldn't even see the landing from the takeoff.] My eagerness to learn was quickly replaced with fear. The only thing worse than false faith is blind faith! This felt like both.

I'd always taken great pride in confronting my fears and moving ahead, but this was a level of fear unlike any other I'd ever faced. Before committing to anything, Jimmy and I made sure our new friend knew that we had only started riding that day, so he slowed down and started with an introduction: his name was Steve Harris. Then he began to share a few critical techniques, rules, and insights to help us remain upright on our bikes and navigate the course. More importantly, he rattled off a list of critical mistakes that would guarantee, if not a broken bone, at least an unprecedented level of embarrassment. He had our attention.

Steve told us, "Lean forward, with your face over the number plate and your eyes up. Grip the bike firmly with your legs, but relax your hands and body to absorb impact smoothly. Tension is your worst enemy, and where your head and eyes go, so do you . . . so don't look down!" The sheer terror I was feeling must have been showing, because he then assured us that with proper alignment and balance, coupled with the appropriate speed, launching and landing a motocross bike "would be a piece of cake and smooth as butter in the sun." A funny way to put it, I thought, but his advice soon proved true.

I tried to follow his instructions on a few short jumps and quickly caught on as Steve promised. Jim and I went home quite dirty and stinky, but all in one piece and feeling like we had accomplished something worthwhile. That day started my love affair with dirt biking, and little did Steve know how he had changed my life by reminding me I could overcome fear and successfully do something completely new to me. He and I are lifelong friends today, really more like brothers—over twenty years later. Thank goodness I mustered the courage to ask for help and not worry about whether a seasoned expert would shun or belittle me.

If you bother to look and have the courage to ask, you can almost always find a role model to answer your questions and help pull you over the big jumps along the way. Someone else's positive reinforcement is often a perfect antidote for your negative thoughts and limiting beliefs. They can help you look farther down the road of success and think bigger thoughts as you plan your future. And remember, a question unasked is a question unanswered.

It always helps to know the rules and strategies involved with any area for growth and development. Wise people learn to use those hacks and cheats to stay ahead of the competition. In my company we call that practice R&D—not "Research and Development," but "Rip-off and Deploy!" Trust me, you can find countless successful experts who would love to share their cheats and hacks with you and help you succeed as they have done. (I'll share many of mine in later chapters.) You just need to ask and then reciprocate with a grateful heart. People who see life as "giving more than you take" will give you their best advice. In that way, you're not ripping off anything or anyone; you're accepting a gift, which is rewarding for them and you.

We all have stories we tell ourselves. If you tell yourself you can do something, you probably can. If you tell yourself you can't do something, you probably can't (or won't). And I've noticed people often confuse "can't" with "won't" to avoid the effort, risk and potential failure. Either way, those stories are like movies we play in our heads. Those stories shape how you see yourself, how you relate to others, your perspective on your capacity to succeed, personal worthiness and even how you relate to money. Pay attention to the stories you tell yourself, and remember that they often aren't the real YOU. Your real story is about your amazing strengths and great potential. We often need other people who are operating at a higher level to objectively critique our stories. Those people can then help us validate the ones that are beneficial and replace the others with stories that inspire and motivate us. That's how I grew into a better musician. It's how my business became much more profitable and fulfilling. It's even how I got more proficient at motorcycle riding. Whenever I've allowed others to help me think bigger and look farther down the road, they propelled me to new levels of success I would never have reached on my own. Find people who can do the same for you. And stop telling yourself who you *aren't* and what you *can't* do . . . at least until you've given 100% of your effort to the cause.

QUESTIONS TO CONSIDER:

1. Who is someone who influenced your childhood plans and dreams (perhaps by completely redirecting them) whose advice turned out to be good and beneficial for you? What did the person help you learn about yourself?

2. Who have been some of your most influential mentors—not just in business, but in all aspects of your life? What did you learn from each one?

3. When have you felt like a small fish in a big pond, suddenly aware of how little you knew in contrast to the others in the group? How did you handle the situation? (Did you keep silent? Try to fake it? Determine to learn all you could from the others? Etc.)

4. On a scale of 1 (not at all) to 10 (totally and completely), how willing are you to ask others for help? Explain your answer.

5. Have you ever had "a Roger Bannister moment" when you suddenly realized (or proved) that you *could* do that amazing feat or reach that ambitious goal that others felt was impossible? Describe the circumstances and how you felt.

6. What are some stories currently playing in your mind that affect how you feel about yourself? Which ones are inspiring you to look farther and think bigger? Which ones need to be deleted and replaced?

CHAPTER 4

YOUR FIRST TWO QUESTIONS

Let's say you need to locate a business you've never been to before, or visit a friend in a city you're not familiar with, or find the nearest Taco Bell for lunch. How do you get there?

Most people these days would simply key an address into a software systems like Waze or Google Maps and follow the step-by-step directions to get there: "Turn left at the next intersection. Go three miles on Highway 40. Get off at Exit 3. Your destination is on the right." Literally no thinking is involved. You blindly trust that, somehow, twenty-four satellites out in space are going to direct you straight to that chalupa supreme you're craving.

GPS is an amazing feature of modern travel. It's easy to just enter our destination and sit back and follow the prompts. However, maybe a little thought *should* be involved at times. Stories abound of people who blindly trusted their GPS and went exactly where that little voice told them to go, even when an ounce of logic should have convinced them to reconsider that advice. Why else would people willingly drive into a lake . . . or the Pacific Ocean . . . or along a section of railroad tracks . . . or down concrete steps in the middle of a busy city . . . or up a mountain goat trail?

I use Google Maps and Waze like everyone else, but I also still love old-school maps which allow you to see the bigger picture. Conversely, GPS-based navigation is very specific and designed to get you to your destination using the most direct route with limited perspective. It effectively eliminates the option of going slightly out of your way to see things that might enhance the experience of a road trip. A map, on the other hand, alerts me to nearby parks, lakes, or other attractions that might be worth my time to see while I'm in the neighborhood. Or I might be fascinated by certain architecture or landscape when I'm in certain areas and decide to take a few minutes to wander around.

I also have an affinity for globes. They remind me that wherever I am at the moment, and no matter what I happen to be seeing, my perspective is only a very small part of a much bigger and broader reality.

That said, GPS is often a lifesaver for most of us at times. That cellphone in your purse or pocket is as powerful as the most robust computer was a few short years ago. With an internet connection, there's virtually nothing you can't find or confirm. GPS even calculates alternative routes if you run into heavy traffic, an unexpected accident, or roadwork.

But despite all its benefits, GPS-based navigation has one limiting shortcoming: it has to know where you are. You can be perfectly precise about where you want to go, but if your phone or car's GPS can't locate you, you're out of luck! It's like the old joke about the salesman desperately lost out in the country who stops to ask directions from a farmer. The local farmer scratches his head as he thinks, and finally determines, "You can't get there from here."

If you're out in the country and find yourself in a cellphone dead zone, you're out of luck. When that happens, you have only two choices: drive around randomly, hoping to wander through an area with cellphone coverage; or sit where you are and hope it finds you. I don't recommend sitting still very long, just wishing your situation would get better. But then, speeding off in the wrong direction isn't any better. That's where good old-fashioned maps and road signs come in handy. It's also a smart idea to plan your trip in advance whenever possible, just in case you find yourself without your usual means of navigation.

WHERE ARE YOU?

Navigating a reasonably straight path to success in your business, family life, or any other worthwhile pursuit is much like using your GPS to go from one point to another. You start by determining, "Where am I?" And then you clarify, "Where do I want to go?" It's that simple . . . and that hard. Actually, answering those two questions isn't usually as easy as it sounds. For example, I sometimes ask young people, "Where do you want to go in life? What do you want to accomplish?" And immediately, off the top of their head, with little if any thought, they respond with some version of "I want to be rich and/or famous." That's about as precise as keying in "Earth" as a destination on your GPS. But we'll look at that second question a bit later. Let's start with the first one.

Step one when embarking on a journey is to confirm exactly where you are. Where are you . . . in life? What are your skills, desires, dreams, passions? Looking back, what are your accomplishments to date? How satisfied would you say you are with all aspects of your life: physical, spiritual, emotional, vocational, financial, etc.? Can you even pinpoint where you are now, or do you seem to be endlessly wandering?

In determining where you are, it's vital to take resources into account. Start with the obvious things you might think of: capital/money, credit, access to people with money to invest, and so forth. But also consider your core genius and gifts—those intangible resources that distinguish you from the rest of the herd on the pathway to success.

If you need a little assistance answering this first question, you'll find numerous tools to help you get started. Here are just a few:

The Myers-Briggs Type Indicator (MBTI)

This Myers-Briggs assessment tool has long been a standard to help clarify your own personality type, which in turn helps you better understand how you relate to various people with other types. The assessment will determine your preferences in four primary categories:

- How you direct and receive energy (Extraversion [E] or Introversion [I]);

- How you take in information (Sensing [S] or Intuition [N]);

- How you make decisions and come to conclusions (Thinking [T] or Feeling [F]); and

- How you approach the outside world (Judging [J] or Perceiving [P]).

More than eighty-eight percent of Fortune 500 companies use this assessment. If you've never taken it, it's an excellent starting point.

The DiSC Assessment

The DiSC model begins with an assessment to provide a common language for people who work together. It helps you determine your personal profile with a goal of better understanding and working with others (resolving conflict, improving teamwork, etc.). The DiSC acronym stands for four primary personality categories: Dominance, Influence, Steadiness, and Conscientiousness. Tony Robbins offers a free version of this assessment on his website (tonyrobbins.com/disc/).

Standout 2.0

I highly recommend the book by this title by Marcus Buckingham. The subtitle says it all: "Assess your strengths, find your edge, win at work." Buckingham's focus is identifying your dominant strengths and then building on them. He also provides readers an online assessment that comes with the book.

The Keller Personality Assessment

Anyone affiliated with my company, Keller Williams Realty, including our clients and friends, has access to this free assessment tool. It's designed to help people see where their personality and approach to work life fit into the real estate industry, including ancillary roles like marketing, accounting, and sales. It's a proprietary assessment KW owns and provides to agents in the Keller Williams Company worldwide in an effort to help self-assess. We also use it in the hiring process of qualifying a candidate to a key role on a team.

These are just a few of the many self-assessment tools available to help you answer your "Where am I?" question. They'll all help you better distinguish and define your distinctive characteristics, natural preferences, and strengths. When determining personality types, there is no right or wrong, yet it can be incredibly helpful to begin to see just how differently from you that some people see the world.

Still, these assessments are just starting points. In my experience, they don't accurately acknowledge raw intelligence, ethical boundaries, work ethic, work history, and personal tenacity. You may not naturally be a motivating leader, or even the sharpest knife in the drawer, yet these other factors can more than compensate. Use those scientific, research-based assessments to help you see more clearly who you are, but don't let them define you!

Just because it turns out you can do something well doesn't necessarily mean that's what you should decide to do for the rest of your life. Your natural abilities may be a clue to an ideal career path, but not necessarily. Conversely, you may *want* to do something passionately, but lack the required skills. You can achieve essentially anything in life, but if you don't have the natural aptitude to do whatever it is you desperately desire to do, it becomes a constant battle to keep trying to improve your performance, work though other people, and so forth. Stress accumulates quickly in such cases. You might want to seriously consider a career in an area where your natural abilities abound, and then pursue your other passions as a hobby.

Let me give you a personal example. I think I could be a decent computer programmer with proper training. I likely have the necessary core skills to master it, but I don't have the passion for it. I am definitely a people-oriented guy, and that's not going to change. So even though I love a good puzzle and technical challenge, I can see how it would tax me at an insane level to spend hours in complete silence and isolation doing the complex thinking required for programming. But if I still wanted to work around computers, my natural wiring would make me an asset at a computer company that needed help with branding, marketing, sales, and distribution. It's possible to be a visionary leader using the gifts you have if you're willing to hire excellent people to fill the roles you're not best at. (More on networking later.)

Early in my college career I met with various professors at Georgia State University for feedback about options I should choose as a major. One professor in the English department suggested I pursue a career in journalism, after having graded a few of my papers favorably. I asked about the lifestyle that came with that career choice, and he said, "Oh, the life of a writer is wonderful. You travel the world, meet unique people, attend grand events, and write an account of those moments for others to enjoy vicariously!"

It sounded enticing to travel, meet cool people, and introduce the world to experiences and ideas they had never pondered. Then I asked, "How much do typical journalists make annually?" He was honest:

"Oh, they make very little money. It's all about the journey in that profession, with little financial reward for most." That was a deal-killer for me. As attractive as it sounded to conceive of an original idea and write it up in a way that would inspire people, I knew I was already wired for entrepreneurship. I wanted to conceive of an original idea and make a business out of it, or at least find an existing business and infuse it with new and creative ideas. I ended up choosing a major in business administration with a focus on business management.

Since then, I've learned to ask myself a question to keep steering me in the right direction: *Do I have a committed heart?* I believe I could have succeeded as a journalist. I might even have eked out a living as a computer programmer. But my heart wasn't in either of those options. Ironically, here I sit writing this book some thirty-two years later, exercising a gift my English professor felt I had. When it comes to success, I firmly believe a committed heart won't quit and cannot be denied. The gut check for each of us is: do I have a committed heart for this endeavor?

Looking back, however, I can see I made a good decision in not trying to stake my career on writing. That was confirmed when I made a career move into real estate. It seemed a logical choice because the job combined a personal interest in houses and architecture with the enjoyment I get from solving problems and my natural inclination to help people. And that choice has been confirmed every day since then because my heart is fully committed to what I'm doing. As a bonus, I could still write, blog, and teach as my skills and track record grew— even without a journalism or teaching degree.

Sometimes you don't know with absolute certainty what's best for you until you do the research, learn the required skills, and ultimately take the plunge and see what happens. When you confirm that you made the right decision, there's no feeling like realizing you've found your purpose in the world. And worst case, you learn some lessons about work and life, and better prepare yourself for your next choice and adventure.

Plus, when I found work that I could get excited about because it fit my natural bent, I never had to worry about the financial aspect. In real estate, rewards are nearly limitless in a commissioned role when dealing in very high-ticket items like homes and land. I found success beyond my wildest dreams—in financial security, yes, but even more so in satisfaction with what I was doing and the joy of going to work every day.

That doesn't mean I ever experienced an epiphany of complete clarity and moment of enlightenment. Along the way, I quit more things than I stuck with. My failures outnumbered my successes. The sooner you learn that failing is vital to finding your joy and ultimate success, the sooner you can more forward again. The worst thing you can do is stay where you are, stuck and unmotivated. Far better is to chalk up another failure and take a shot at something else. When you finally arrive at the right thing for you, that final success will immediately make you forget about all those previous failures. André Gide, a French author and winner of the Nobel Prize in Literature, said, "It is better to fail at your own life than to succeed at someone else's." That's a crucial statement. Take a moment and let it sink in. Get real with yourself and make the statement your mantra going forward.

So . . . are you ready to answer your first personal GPS-coordinate question: *Where are you in terms of your skills, talents, passions, and desires?* Until you have a reliable reading on your starting point, it makes little sense to try to figure out where you're going from there. But when you're ready, feel free to move on to your second question.

WHERE DO YOU WANT TO GO?

Your answer to this question, as with your responses to all the exercises in this book, should be rooted in courageous honesty. Your desired destination should be *your* choice—not your parents', your spouse's, or your coworkers'. If you're always plotting your next step to make someone else happy (or even worse, to try to prove something to your frenemies . . . insincere, shallow, self-appointed friends), you never get around to discovering *your* purpose, contributing *your* intuitive wisdom, living *your* life. Sounds depressing, doesn't it? It is.

The authors of the book, *True Faced,* caution their readers: "All of us need to be able to recognize our patterns of hiding. We need to understand how wearing a mask has affected our relationships and frustrated our maturing and influence."

If you've been wearing a mask, it is essential that you take it off at once and reveal to the world who you really are. You will never regret the time you spend in a clear-minded consideration of where you are and where *you* want to go. You were born with a brain and a heart connected to a voice inside of you that's like a compass constantly seeking true north. At times, a compass is more important than GPS to determine the general direction leading to fulfillment. As you'll see in the next section of this chapter, there are twelve categories in the Life Wheel, and in each category, you'll find clarity for your true north, but only if you pause and analyze it with an open mind. You'll then be able to chart your course in each area of your personal road map (using a personal GPS in this analogy) to create a turn-by-turn plan to achieve all of your goals. A life with no regrets begins by pursuing your own song, your own dreams, and your own goals—and not settling for anything less. Seriously, "No RAGRETS" . . . not even a letter!

For the past decade, I have led a workshop called, "Your Future Self." I walk men and women of all ages and stages in life through the steps of projecting their "five-year-future self" all the way to their "fifty-year-future self." It's a powerful and practical way to help participants answer the "Where do you want to go?" question, both in the short-term and long-term. It also helps them determine, "Who do you want to become as a human being?" It's holistic and all-encompassing of key areas of life.

I always enjoy leading the Future Self workshop because I remember the impact it had on me as I began my career. In 1996, I was thirty years old with a new career in real estate, a relatively new marriage, building a new home, and had a new baby on the way . . . as I was moving into a one hundred percent commissioned job. Failure was not an option. I was committed to outworking and outhustling everyone else to get ahead; however, at that point in my life, I suffered a noticeable imbalance in pursuit of success as I tried to build something from the ground up. For that reason, I sometimes fell short in important areas of life because I was preoccupied with some things and unaware of others.

I had learned the real estate scripts and chosen some of the best role models possible, but my big breakthrough came with this Future Self exercise. I was attending a class about how to hire the right person for the right position, and one aspect of the hiring process was to understand where the candidate sees himself or herself in the next five years.

To qualify us to help a new employee envision his or her "future self," Bev Steiner first took class members through the process for ourselves. She was truly masterful. We started with a personality assessment tool to determine whether the candidate was a match for the job or had abilities better suited for a different position. Step two was an in-depth list of key questions challenging the candidate to reveal life experiences and perspective. Next was a job-by-job review of the candidate's résumé. Then came the "future self" conversation, and the workshop closed with expectations for the candidate, a job description discussion, and the actual agreement to go into business together.

Bev told us all to find a partner and ask each other questions to help one another clarify where we wanted to be in the next five years. My partner that day was Mike Tavener, a friend and great real estate professional who had driven down for the class from North Carolina. Bev guided us smoothly through the whole process, but it was the time spent envisioning myself five years from now that resonated with me that day—and continues to do so. Mike and I created our vision boards in a matter of thirty minutes.

Who knew that a half-hour could change my life in such a powerful way? I suddenly had a holistic view of my entire life and future. It was a new, big vision to focus on and grow into as I continued my journey.

In those thirty minutes, I decided that I wanted to have ownership in seven Keller Williams offices. I had already planned to open my second office that year, but that day I decided to set the goal of one more per year for five consecutive years. This process required me to consider "why" this goal was important. It became clear that the outcome was to not only build a powerful company with amazing people, but also to create a built-in platform for teaching and training, something I was (and am) incredibly passionate about.

YOU'VE LIKELY HEARD THE SAYING, "WHEN YOU OPERATE IN YOUR STRENGTH ZONE WHERE PASSION NATURALLY LIVES, YOU'LL NEVER TRULY WORK A DAY OF YOUR LIFE."

I also made the conscious decision to live more purposefully and give more attention to my relationships, health, epic travel, and more. I wanted to learn more so I could become a better teacher, and I wanted to devote more of my time to help the less fortunate in downtown Atlanta. I set simple, reasonable goals in every area of my life. I didn't think too hard about strategies at that point; I just allowed the vision to flow onto my paper as Mike asked each question. It was inspiring to see them show up in oversized print, with a degree of permanence as I fearlessly projected out five years from that moment. It didn't have to happen that day, that month, or even that year, so surely I could figure it out over the long haul, and the goals were awesome!

I had no idea that little exercise would set my life on a course to so much more success. There was something magical about declaring where you are going and being bold enough to write it down. My plan was not artistic or crafty, but it reflected what I truly wanted in every area of my life. It got my blood racing and sparked what eventually became this book. As I interviewed hundreds of candidates for countless roles over the years, I began to pay more attention to things I could share or ask that would create a safe environment for them to be more honest about their real hopes and dreams—not just what they thought the interviewer wanted to hear.

Later I discovered Henriette Anne Klauser's book, *Write It Down, Make It Happen.* She explains how simply writing down your goals is the first step toward achieving them. I agree! It is not enough to hold those dreams in your mind. Writing them down and looking at them daily will transform your life. It helped me identify and stay focused on the things that were truly important to me.

THE LIFE WHEEL

I got so much from this exercise that I've crafted a template to help people I consult with—and now I'll share with you. It's called the Life Wheel. The original concept was created by the late Paul J. Meyer, who founded the Success Motivation Institute® in 1960. Today, different variations of the wheel are used by coaches and those in the personal development space. After coaching and consulting for many years, I've expanded it to twelve categories because I believe more detail helps people clarify their current status and future goals. This is how it works: You rate each category on a scale of 1 to 10, where 1 means you are completely unsatisfied and fall short constantly. A 10 means you are living your dream in that area. If you don't relate at all to one (or more) of the categories, then just dismiss it and move on, or replace it with something important in your life that didn't get included on the wheel.

In using this wheel with people from various age-groups and careers, essentially all of them want to see varying degrees of improvement in specific facets of their life. For example, one person may want to see slight improvement in her relationship with her friends, but desires a lot of improvement to her health. Someone else's career might be going well, but he realizes his marriage and personal life need some major changes. You might also find your financial situation is being compromised, but you rate your hobbies and travel categories a 10, causing some imbalance and conflict with your total well-being.

Before you start filling in numbers, keep a few things in mind. This first step isn't an exact science; it's just a starting point. Don't overthink it. Just go with how you feel in your gut about each of the categories. The purpose is not to pass judgment in any way, but rather to provide you with a snapshot of overall satisfaction and reveal where you need the most work.

Also, this exercise is to clarify how *you* feel about yourself. Some people may think you're a genius in some of these areas; others may think you're the world's biggest loser. It doesn't matter what either group thinks. Be honest with yourself, because you're the only one who will ultimately have regrets if you don't live your own life.

With these caveats in mind, take a moment to rate your personal satisfaction in each area. Enter your numbers in the blanks below, or go to RickHale.com to download the PDFs for this section.

Before you begin, let me give you some encouragement:

- Be ruthlessly honest. It doesn't help to try to fool yourself (or others) about how you're doing, but being honest also means you should appreciate your strengths and the progress you've made.

- Don't judge your insides by other people's outsides. If you look too often at postings on Facebook or Instagram, you'll assume you're a loser! They're posing.

- Be realistic. Don't compare yourself to individuals who are the very best in a category. They're so focused on one goal that they probably are severely deficient in a few others.

- When you're finished with each area, connect the dots to see what your wheel (or some other geometric design!) looks like. This enables you to notice where the wheel is out of balance.

- Don't settle for average! In the most important aspects of your life, five isn't an option. Determine the areas that are your priorities, and focus on improving those.

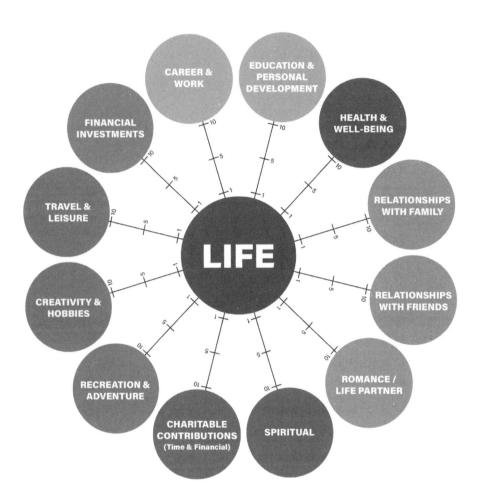

LIFE WHEEL

Starting from the center, rank each area of your life on a scale from 1 to 10, with 10 being perfect. Draw a circle and connect your ranking dots to complete your current Life Wheel. This will show areas you need/desire to balance.Back to Your Two Questions

After rating each category in your Life Wheel, you should have a pretty good snapshot of where you are now. Cumulatively, those scores equate to the starting point on your GPS—indicated by a green dot on most apps. They also provide a good baseline to help answer your second question: *Where do you want to go?*

Think about it this way: If you stay on the exact same path, where will that path take you in the next five, ten, and twenty years? For example, if you keep the same habits, what will your health look like in five years . . . or in two decades? What kind of financial shape will you be in? What will your relationships look like? What does your *best life ever* look like?

I was at a party recently when a man, who looked like he was in his early 60s, told me this story. He said, "Eight years ago my wife and I were doing our usual evening routine—ignoring one another while staring blankly at the TV. We'd been married for thirty years. A late-night infomercial came on claiming that the average lifespan is now eighty-three years. I looked at my wife and said, 'I don't think I want to be with you for another thirty-three years.' She said, 'I agree. You're no cup of tea, either. Why don't we call it a day?' We called the divorce lawyers the next morning."

In Ernest Hemingway's *The Sun Also Rises*, a character asks another how he found himself bankrupt, and he astutely replied, "Two ways, gradually, then suddenly." That's the same way relationships tend to erode. Are you seeing signs that you're growing in the relationship area (and all the others) on your Life Wheel? If they're not growing, they may be slowly dying. Commit to growth. Frankly, all facets of the wheel almost always improve (or fail) gradually, and then suddenly. Darren Hardy speaks to this phenomenon in his book *The Compound Effect,* and it's also engrained in the content found in Seth Godin's book *Drip*—both are great reads. Gradual movement can build momentum

YOUR FIRST TWO QUESTIONS | 93

and lead to sudden unexpected outcomes, especially as it pertains to habits of health, relationships, and money management.

If you knew you had only one more year to live, what changes would you make? Then again, what if you knew for sure you'd live another thirty, forty, or fifty years? Are you already among the crowd who has started settling for less just because they've reached a certain age? As with all important areas of life—you make your choices and then your choices make you.

Take a moment to go back through each category on the wheel, this time projecting your future based on your current routines. Make your best estimate as to where your current internal GPS is leading you, and again assign 1 to 10 scores, this time for your projected five-year-future self if things *don't* change. This is the equivalent of your desired destination on your GPS—the red dot on your app. As you look more intentionally into your future, where are you going? Are you satisfied with your direction and progress? If not, now is the time to start making some changes.

With your five-year-future scores in mind, view the connected dots on your Life Wheel as a car tire. What kind of balance does it have? Is it round or lopsided? Maybe it looks like a starfish! Are a lot of very positive nines and tens offset by twos and threes in other categories? Those are flat spots on your wheel. If so, you're in for a relatively rough ride until you establish more balance. You simply can't speed up and think you'll magically enjoy a silky-smooth ride. It's very rare for someone to score nines and tens in every category, but that's a realistic *long-term goal* for success. And it's very common to have flat spots on your wheel today. The key is to recognize and course-correct as soon as possible. Step 1 is awareness. A life without regrets requires that all aspects are at an acceptable and healthy level.

Don't become overly concerned at this point if your numbers aren't as high as you wish. We'll soon see what you can do to bring them up.

Andy Stanley wrote a book titled *The Principle of the Path*. His observation was that we're all on a path that's leading us somewhere. And no self-help book or motivational speech can help us unless we choose to get off that path and start in a new direction. I created the Life Wheel in hopes of helping more people see how to get off a path of mediocrity, or even potential harm, and find instead a road to long-term growth and fulfillment.

This exercise provides you the opportunity to look down the road. Think. Meditate. Pray. I even ask God, "Lord, show me where this path is taking me. Reveal the danger I'm too foolish to see. Open my eyes to the opportunities I'm missing on my current path. Give me a vision of a new path." When I listen closely, real insight almost always shows up. And if it scares me a little but I still know it's what I need, it's probably a really good path!

First determine, "Where do I want to go?" Then consider what's been keeping you from getting there. Whatever your past issues have been (laziness, distraction, quitting prematurely, blaming others, etc.), determine what you can and cannot control. If it's something you can't control, stop blaming yourself. If it's a problem you can do something about and haven't yet, stop letting yourself off the hook. If you aren't sure about what is in your scope of control, ask a wise counselor to provide some insight and give you accurate context for your decisions.

Steven Pressfield wrote, "The difference between a professional and an amateur is in their habits. An amateur has amateur habits. A professional has professional habits. We can never free ourselves from habits. The human being is a creature of habit. If you're in pursuit of a better you in any category, then frankly, the habits and perspective that got you *here* won't get you *there*! But we can replace bad habits with good ones."[1]

If you start today to improve your regular habits, or perhaps begin some, you can vastly improve your projected score for your five-year-future self. A slight change of habits in just a few areas can make a surprisingly significant difference in arriving at balance and satisfaction with life.

And don't be too quick to put away your Life Wheel. You'll need it as we continue this process in the next chapter.

QUESTIONS TO CONSIDER:

1. Have you ever taken a self-assessment test to discover more about your specific skills and/or interests? If so, what did you discover about yourself? If not, it will be worth your time to ask around, see what's available to you, and see which one(s) others recommend.

2. Have you ever had a job you were really good at, yet had no passion for? What made you decide to leave? (Or are you still there?)

3. Did your Life Wheel exercises reveal anything unexpected about where you are now? How did you feel about the projected scores for your five-year-future self?

4. Now that you're plotting a path from where you are to where you want to go, are you ready to choose to do whatever it takes to get there? Why or why not?

CHAPTER 5

THE PATH TO YOUR FIVE-YEAR-FUTURE SELF

Perhaps you've worked for a company, attended a church, or been involved with another organization that had a mission statement and/or a vision statement. The mission statement tends to be a down-to-earth document that seeks to ensure that all the members of the organization are on the same page and working toward the same goal. The individuals can be there for all kinds of different reasons, but the mission statement points them in the same direction.

The vision statement, in contrast, is inspirational and motivational. Laurie Beth Jones defines it as "the end result of what you will have done. It is a picture of how the landscape will look after you've been through it. It is your 'ideal'." Then she provides a couple of examples to illustrate the difference between mission and vision:

It was the vision of Christopher Columbus returning to Spain with ships full of spices, converts, and gold that led Queen Isabella to grant him the money for the journey. She surely would not have granted him the funds if he had approached her with "I need three ships, lots of men, lots of money, lots of time, and maybe I'll get back to you." This was actually the *reality* of the situation, yet Columbus sold her on the vision first. The details became almost insignificant.

The founding fathers who met in Philadelphia envisioned "a more perfect union based on life, liberty, and the pursuit of happiness." They did not write down "We are going to lose our land, our lives, our fortunes, and everything we've worked for while trudging through mud, enduring freezing cold, and dying from lead bullets." This was the reality of what happened to many of them. Yet it was the vision of a free land, shimmering in the not too distant future, which kept them loading their muskets and pushing their mules and eating hard tack and sipping soup.[2]

Many people are confused about these concepts, so let me clarify them: A vision statement is *future-oriented and aspirational*. It identifies the values and purpose of the individual, family, or organization . . . the big picture, the end result. A mission statement is *present-oriented, identifying clear goals* and focusing on the specific steps to achieve them. You might think of it as the introduction to your goals.

Although vision statements are customary for most organizations, it's far less common to meet *individuals* who have crafted a personal vision that's distinguishable from their specific, immediate and long-term goals. Your vision statement should capture your intentions for your life as a whole, the impact you hope to have, the legacy you plan to leave to others. And if you have a family, it's powerful for families to come together to define a unified and family mission and vision statements.

This is exactly how your life's vision, mission and goals are like a GPS—they get you where you want to go! Do you use your GPS ap when you drive a few blocks to a restaurant or to your office? No, probably not. Do you use it if you're traveling to another city? Yes, even if you've driven there a hundred times, you still want to know if there are any traffic problems you need to avoid. What if I wanted to drive from Atlanta to Seattle? I'd certainly use it! It may give me several options so I can choose the quickest or most scenic route, and I keep checking it all along the way to see if I've been rerouted away from trouble. A short trip or a long one, it's important to use excellent navigation.

After you have a carefully written vision and mission statements, it's time to identify your goals. Goal-setting is very important, so much so that essentially every self-help book proposes a different take on how it should be done. As you try to incorporate everyone's suggestions, the process can become frustrating and tedious—like attempting to solve a complex math equation. As a result, our goals are often uninspired and unfulfilling, focused more on "getting the formula right" rather than achieving the heightened clarity and personal satisfaction of knowing we're getting closer to what we believe to be our purpose on earth.

One of the most helpful tools to find clarity in goals is a framework called "SMART goals." For each element of your Life Wheel, write (and rewrite) goals that are:

- *Specific:* Broad, vague goals won't get you where you want to go. Be narrow, and clearly define each one.

- *Measurable:* What metrics will show progress toward the goal?

- *Attainable:* Boldness is a virtue, but setting goals that are too high inevitably leads to discouragement.

- *Relevant:* Your goals need to align with your vision (your values and aspirations).

- *Time-based:* In a sense, you're delegating your future to yourself, and in delegation, the most helpful question is: "Who does what by when?" A firm deadline sharpens thinking, clarifies priorities, and encourages action.[3]

I encourage people to distinguish between goals and intentions as a good starting place to identify goals that are aligned with your vision statement. By definition, a goal is the object of a person's ambition, an aim or desire in the future. It's most often viewed as a destination or outcome, but it may lack the power of intrinsic motivation—which come from the intentions of our hearts. I define *intentions* in this context as how you expect to feel when you accomplish your goals and why it matters. A well-conceived intention explains *why* the goal is important to you. Your defined "why" is a powerful force to maintain commitments, motivation and perseverance! And the "why" for each category will support your mission and vision statement. A strong "why" will also compel others to join you because they realize their involvement aligns with their mission and vision, too.

In a brilliant TED talk, Simon Sinek connected the dots between the "why" and the "what," especially for corporate leaders but also for leaders in any organization, including parents. He observes, "People don't buy WHAT you do, they buy WHY you do it. . . . The role of a leader is not to come up with all the great ideas. The role of a leader is to create an environment in which great ideas can happen. . . . Working hard for something we do not care about is called stress, working hard for something we love is called passion."[4] As we chart our future and communicate what's important to us, we need to articulate the "why" even more than the "what." "Why" is vision; "what" is mission and goals.

It's natural to assume your goal will fulfill your intentions, but that just isn't always the case. I don't know about you, but I used to set goals without real purpose or accountability attached to them. I found that if I'm not clear on the intentions for certain goals, meeting those goals may turn out to be unsatisfying—only a distraction from what I might have accomplished had I started with a clearer vision of my intentions.

Let's consider health as an example. I am one of many people who set health-oriented goals like regular exercise, eating nutritious foods, and getting quality sleep nightly. Those are all clear and measurable ambitions, yet it's often hard to stay motivated and on course with only a stand-alone "goal." But suppose I add an intention that's personal to me, like, "I want to live a healthy life free of pain and physically capable of keeping up with grandchildren one day!" Suddenly, the idea of sticking to my diet and getting out of bed earlier to exercise becomes much more appealing. If you do the same with every aspect of your life, your motivation for personal growth and purposeful living increases exponentially.

Accomplishing goals without connecting them to well-conceived intentions can create more frustration than satisfaction. How many people do you know who finally meet their long-term goal of acquiring a fancy sports car or completing an expensive house remodel, only to discover that afterward they aren't any happier? Did they never ask, "Why did I have that sports car on my dream list to begin with?" or "What was driving my desire for a nicer house?" In retrospect, it may be that some of the things they sacrificed to meet those goals (time, resources, family involvement, etc.) would ultimately have been more fulfilling.

A clearer vision of meaningful intentions will help us improve our goals. The key is to start with intentions that demand high expectations but yield high personal reward as a result. Then, if you're true to your intentions, your goals can be modified or recalibrated to adjust to changing circumstances and lead to better results.

YOUR GOALS AND INTENTIONS

In the previous chapter, you gave each category of your Life Wheel a 1 to 10 score. You rated yourself in each category at this moment *if things don't change.* This is the point where you see how new goals and clear intentions can make a major difference in your future. It's a time to be authentic and honest, but also zealously ambitious and realistically hopeful. I want you to set some thoughtfully considered goals, but I want you to give your intentions even higher priority. In other words, give yourself the freedom to create some passionate expectations without knowing exactly how you'll accomplish them.

Goals are the *what*, and intentions are the *why*. It's important to think through both of them at the same time. Start with the Life Wheel you completed. On the Goals and Intentions Worksheet write a goal beside each category that you hope to reach within the next five years— where you *want* to be—and look beneath the surface to tap into your real motivation to reach that goal. (Later, you can begin to schedule those goals into your day planner and start working toward them as soon as possible. After you put them in the schedule, you might be surprised at how motivated you will become.)

Let's use the Health & Fitness category as an example again. If I want to raise my score to a 9 or 10, my goal would be to reach peak fitness for a person my age. My regimen might include: riding my bike fifteen to twenty miles weekly; weight lifting three times a week; doing 100 sit-ups, pushups, and squats daily with a trainer (in person or virtual); appropriate seasonal exercise each week (motocross, tennis, snowboarding, wakeboarding, wake surfing, etc.); intermittent fasting and consistent healthy food choices; involvement in yoga and other stretching classes for flexibility; and a minimum of seven to eight hours of sleep every night.

Please note: these are *my* goals based on *my* definition of what a Level 10 would look like in my life. My personal trainer would probably have other ideas, as would my friends and family. But if I want to reach the highest levels of achievement in all these areas of my life,

I can't be overly concerned about what everybody else thinks. You shouldn't, either. Write out your goals describing what will make *you* feel completely fulfilled.

For this exercise, identify your "why"—your intention for each category. Pick one or two activities you can accomplish with ease in each category. The idea is to get your creative juices going that will lead you to next-level goals to move you toward your five-year-future self. Use SMART goals, and define those you could do in the next week or two, certainly within the month. Write them down. Again, this will be the launching pad for your five-year-future-self exercise still to come.

On your Goals and Intentions Worksheet (found a few pages later in this chapter), record some goals for each of the categories that you believe would get you to improve a number or two in the short term to get you started on your five-year journey to 9's and 10's. And spend time considering the why, your motivation, the real payoff that will drive you toward each goal. Don't be in a hurry. It often takes time to discover our deeper desires, but it's time well spent. Imagine how you perceive your life would look in each area if you were living at Level 10. Write with a stream-of-consciousness mindset, without editing. Allow yourself to imagine each area from every angle. Don't worry about impressing anyone or trying to fit into a mold; instead, write what you would like to feel and what you would like to experience if each of your intentions were fully realized.

Start with these questions to get your mind churning, and add other observations of your own:

- Why is it important to you to reach this level? (I believe that if the *why* is important enough, the *how* will come to you.)

- How would you view your life differently at level 10? What habits will be different?

- What accomplishments will you have made by then that you haven't yet achieved?

- Who benefits from your success?

- What are the mechanics or the processes necessary for success?

- How will you feel when you accomplish it?

Resist the impulse to merely answer these questions to fill in the blanks. You're not being graded. Neatness doesn't count. At this stage you should be writing in block paragraphs, as quickly as possible, challenging your pen to keep up with the ideas flowing from your mind. (The next step will be crystallizing and clarifying the best ideas. Don't let that slow you down here.)

I already shared with you my *goals* in the Health and Fitness category. Here is what my *intentions* paragraph looks like—the ideals that will help me stick to those goals:

At Level 10 I will feel lean, strong, and able to enjoy an active life for myself and family. I'll be enhancing the odds I'll live a long life, one that includes quality time with grandkids that don't even exist yet. I'll be in a healthy state where I'm able to minimize physical limitations and pain. I will be a role model for my kids as they begin to enjoy and embrace the challenges of aging. I'm a consistent encourager for my wife and not a burden on her as we both age gracefully.

In summary, after identifying your current 1-10 score for each category, set SMART goals and clarify your intention for each category. Then list one or two short-term goals that will move the rating closer to a 10. A short-term goal is one you can accomplish in 30 days or less ... and perhaps even sooner, in a week or two. Accomplishing this goal will probably move your category rating only one number better, but this progress is significant because it's one number closer to your long-term goals (which you'll work on in the next exercise). And remember, your 10 is your own ideal, not the world's version you've see on social media. This step is intended to help you clarify your "why" for each category. It's a practice run at a few goals and activities to initiate positive momentum. After this section we'll move to the next step that looks out five years and beyond.

Pro Tip: Set an appointment in your day planner/calendar for any short-term goal that needs immediate attention. If it's important, it should always be in your day planner. If you set the appointment and make it non-negotiable, it'll get done.

And remember, if a category has little relevance in the current moment, don't get hung up trying to make it something it's not. Avoid setting short-term goals that don't align with long-term intentions.

Keep an open mind and realize an amazing "perfect you" might shift over time due to life experiences, external circumstances beyond your control and lessons you learn from your experiences. I have a good friend and educator at Keller Williams named Dick Dillingham who once advised me, "Stay KOOL!" It's an acronym for Keen Observer of Life. He's right—the key to self-awareness and personal growth is recognizing things around you that enable instead of disable . . . and leaning into the positive ones. Stay KOOL!

Dive into the Goals and Intentions Worksheet (you can use the one in the book or download a larger version at RickHale.com), and get your wheels spinning in the right direction! Craft a short description of the ideal, set a couple of goals, clarify "why" the category matters and then write them in your day planner.

Think. Write. Repeat.

GOALS AND INTENTIONS WORKSHEET

(You can download a copy at RickHale.com.)

Spiritual

Current score:

Your goal, or what a 10 might look like in five years:

What difference will achieving these goals make? (This is your passionate intention!)

One or two specific, immediate goals that will move you forward in the next 30 in days or less:

Health & Well-Being

Current score:

Your goal, or what a 10 might look like in five years:

What difference will achieving these goals make? (This is your passionate intention!)

One or two specific, immediate goals that will move you forward in the next 30 in days or less:

Relationships with Family

Current score:

Your goal, or what a 10 might look like in five years:

What difference will achieving these goals make? (This is your passionate intention!)

One or two specific, immediate goals that will move you forward in the next 30 in days or less:

Romance/Life Partner
Current score:

Your goal, or what a 10 might look like in five years:

What difference will achieving these goals make? (This is your passionate intention!)

One or two specific, immediate goals that will move you forward in the next 30 in days or less:

Relationships with Friends
Current score:

Your goal, or what a 10 might look like in five years:

What difference will achieving these goals make? (This is your passionate intention!)

One or two specific, immediate goals that will move you forward in the next 30 in days or less:

Education & Personal Development
Current score:

Your goal, or what a 10 might look like in five years:

What difference will achieving these goals make? (This is your passionate intention!)

One or two specific, immediate goals that will move you forward in the next 30 in days or less:

Career & Work

Current score:

Your goal, or what a 10 might look like in five years:

What difference will achieving these goals make? (This is your passionate intention!)

One or two specific, immediate goals that will move you forward in the next 30 in days or less:

Financial Investments

Current score:

Your goal, or what a 10 might look like in five years:

What difference will achieving these goals make? (This is your passionate intention!)

One or two specific, immediate goals that will move you forward in the next 30 in days or less:

Recreation & Adventure

Current score:

Your goal, or what a 10 might look like in five years:

What difference will achieving these goals make? (This is your passionate intention!)

One or two specific, immediate goals that will move you forward in the next 30 in days or less:

Charitable Contributions (Time and Money)

Current score:

Your goal, or what a 10 might look like in five years:

What difference will achieving these goals make? (This is your passionate intention!)

One or two specific, immediate goals that will move you forward in the next 30 in days or less:

Travel & Leisure

Current score:

Your goal, or what a 10 might look like in five years:

What difference will achieving these goals make? (This is your passionate intention!)

One or two specific, immediate goals that will move you forward in the next 30 in days or less:

Creativity & Hobbies

Current score:

Your goal, or what a 10 might look like in five years:

What difference will achieving these goals make? (This is your passionate intention!)

One or two specific, immediate goals that will move you forward in the next 30 in days or less:

By now, I hope you're realizing that this process is more than just a mental exercise. The procedure is a bit demanding, but it can change your life if you're willing to follow through with your ideas as you work toward a much-improved five-year-future self. This process is how you get the information for your GPS so you can chart the best course and stay on it. Your ap does all this for you, but your mentors can help you download the information from your heart.

This exercise gives you permission to dream. Dream of starting a ministry even if your whole world is crumbling around you. Dream of financial security even in the middle of a financial crisis. Dream of a close relationship with your loved one, even if you are currently estranged. Let your dreams lead to decisions that put you on a new path and make you a better, more fulfilled person.

I recently had lunch with Jeff, a friend who told me the story of his life change. Years earlier, his life had been falling apart. He had fallen prey to drugs, been unfaithful to his wife, and suffered a complete emotional and psychological breakdown. He had a very lucrative job, but it was not at all rewarding. Deep down, he knew something—more like everything—had to change.

He began rebuilding, one category at a time, until he created an entirely new life for himself. He now has a ministry for teen boys who don't have strong father figures. He's supported by another committed friend, Greg Washington, who works out of The City of Refuge in Atlanta. He told me, "I want to serve boys who are like me, who don't have a dad or a trustworthy male role model." The day we spoke, he had just completed a weekend retreat through his ministry called "Building Your Legacy."

His ministry logo is a buffalo. He explained that most animals, when they sense a storm coming, find cover away from the wind and rain to escape the inherent danger. They often scatter and run in random directions. But the buffalo herd sticks together, faces the headwinds, and powers through the storm.

Years before, Jeff had been unable to imagine any kind of new and happy life, much less as a leader of a ministry. And above all, he found peace and forgiveness from God and committed himself to a life of purpose. He forgave himself for making selfish decisions and hurting people, and he made amends with those he had hurt. With that, he could experience inner healing so he could again move forward. He took the mindset of *progress, not perfect* as the path to a better version of himself . . . and he went to work! He went from feeling alone and hopeless to experiencing a life of meaning a few short years later.

Positive change begins with the dream, the vision, the idea. Remember, your subconscious mind is a riddle solver and works to answer the questions and challenges you pose. When your desire for change is presented in a positive light, your mind will disclose or devise new life-changing ideas and people to support your goal.

So be bold as you envision your life, category by category, in the immediate and then five years into the future. Write down your intentions. Let the ideas flow, resolutely refusing to edit or compromise during this stage. Don't settle for less.

After you've done all that, you're still not finished. Take another break, if you wish, but hurry back. The best is yet to come.

FIVE-YEAR GOALS

I know that I'm pushing you, but this is important. Dreams and visions won't take you where you want to go if you don't do the hard work to be specific. On the Goals and Intentions worksheet, I asked you to identify some specific goals. Now, I want you to dive in more deeply. It's often helpful to triage the areas of life: your highest priorities, your lowest ones, and those in between. Invest your time, your attention, your passion, and your resources in the highest priorities first.

Begin with the areas that are your highest priorities. What are the steps you need to take to reach your goals in those areas? Write the one or two immediate goals from the Goals and Intentions Worksheet you just completed on the first line or two on the Five-Year Category Goal Worksheet. You may only write one or two more items, or as many as it takes to ensure you're clear about what has to happen in the next five years to achieve your ideal long-term, amazing, future self! Write as many goals as you want to consider, but prioritize the top four in each category. (You can use this worksheet or download a full-scale one at RickHale.com.)

FIVE-YEAR CATEGORY GOAL WORKSHEET

Spiritual

All the goals I'm considering for the next five years:

My top four priorities:

Health & Well-Being

All the goals I'm considering for the next five years:

My top four priorities:

Relationships with Family

All the goals I'm considering for the next five years:

My top four priorities:

Romance/Life Partner

All the goals I'm considering for the next five years:

My top four priorities:

Relationships with Friends

All the goals I'm considering for the next five years:

My top four priorities:

Education & Personal Development

All the goals I'm considering for the next five years:

My top four priorities:

Career & Work

All the goals I'm considering for the next five years:

My top four priorities:

Financial Investments

All the goals I'm considering for the next five years:

My top four priorities:

Recreation & Adventure

All the goals I'm considering for the next five years:

My top four priorities:

Charitable Contributions (Time and Money)

All the goals I'm considering for the next five years:

My top four priorities:

Travel & Leisure

All the goals I'm considering for the next five years:

My top four priorities:

Creativity & Hobbies

All the goals I'm considering for the next five years:

My top four priorities:

CREATE YOUR VISION BOARD

You're ready! All the groundwork is done. You've put pencil to paper to record your best ideas, your most important goals, and a bold vision of your future. It's almost time to put marker to poster board. After a preliminary but crucial exercise, you're going to create a vision board of your five-year-future self. This is the exercise I did at the Future Self Workshop I described in the previous chapter—the thirty minutes that changed my life. I hope it will provide similar results for you.

But it's a little too soon to create your vision board. We're adding another step so you can prioritize your goals one more time. It's better to do a few things really well than try to accomplish a lot of goals and become disillusioned when things don't happen as fast as you'd like! Now, make a practice run. I've created a chart with four quadrants to help you prioritize your goals.

I've taken the liberty of grouping the twelve category goals into four quadrants. These quadrants represent a balanced life. I also recommend you write your favorite motivating affirmation on top of the sheet and date it to show when your "five-year-future self" clock officially started.

The Four Quadrant Grid Worksheet is a tool to identify the specific goals that will go on your vision board. This is a crucial exercise to finalize your top priorities. The instructions for this exercise are:

1. Transfer all of your goals from the Five-Year Goal Worksheet to the Four Quadrant Worksheet. If you have four for each category, you'll have 12 in each quadrant.

2. Take time to prioritize the goals that will create your best self in the next five years. You might have one or two for each category, or you might have more in some categories than others. It's entirely up to you to identify what's most important. For each priority, explain your motivation and the benefits. I recommend this template:

   GOAL: What you want to accomplish.

   What's involved, Who, When (timing: start or completion), and How (if you know).

   Who benefits from accomplishing the goal.

   How you'll feel when you accomplish it!

   For example, my previous vision boards have contained goals like:

- Buy one investment property per year for next five years.

- Spend six weeks on vacation each year.

- Help children in poverty in inner-city Atlanta.

- Perform once a month with my band and write one new song monthly.

- Schedule individual weekly time with each of my kids and one date night with my wife.

- Go to a physical trainer three days per week.

- Live the 70/30 rule monthly, 70% income to lifestyle, 10% charity, 10% savings, 10% investments.

- Network with entrepreneurs to find and share investment opportunities

3. To highlight your intentions and keep your motivation sharp, write an affirmation at the top of the page. Some people will use a Bible passage, others will use a quote from their favorite author, and some will craft their own statement. For instance:

"Now to him who is able to do immeasurably more than all we ask or imagine, according to his power that is at work within us."
—Ephesians 3:20

"Fear not, for I am with you; be not dismayed, for I am your God; I will strengthen you, I will help you, I will uphold you with my righteous right hand."
—Isaiah 41:10

"Success is not final; failure is not fatal: It's the courage to continue that counts."
—Winston Churchill

"It's not the will to win that matters—everyone has that. It's the will to prepare to win that matters."
—Paul "Bear" Bryant

"If it's to be, why not me?"
—Rick Hale

4. After you've finished the first three steps, make a final, clean draft of the worksheet. You'll reproduce this draft in larger form on poster paper.

FOUR-QUADRANT WORKSHEET

Affirmation: Date:

Career & Work, Education & Personal Development, Financial Investments	Relationships with Family, Relationships with Friends, Romance/Life Partner
Spiritual, Health & Well-Being, Charitable Contributions	Travel & Leisure, Creativity & Hobbies, Recreation & Adventure

When you've documented your most important goals on the grid, you're ready to create your vision board! Find markers and a poster board or whiteboard. I recommend buying easel paper with a sticky top from an office supply store. The sticky top will last years and makes hanging it on a wall easy, and it's portable. I also suggest using the gridded option when writing goals on poster paper. I like the Post-It™ brand, but the choice is yours. And you'll need four different colored pens—and always use darker colors, since pastels and light colors tend to fade over time.

Now, reproduce your finalized Four Quadrant Worksheet (from Step 4 in the instructions) onto the poster paper, complete with emojis if that speaks to you, an affirmation, and the date. (When I write them on the poster paper, I make them equidistant with enough space between each goal to write in the supporting information to remind me of not only who, what, when and how (if you know), but also who benefits, and how I'll feel when I accomplish the goal. I like to make each goal the same color so that each goal is very clear. I then stagger the who, what, when or how in another color and the same under each major goal. The idea behind four different colors and staggering the supporting information is that they stand out when you look at it daily and on the run. Don't make your brain work to achieve a clear picture of where you're going with your goals and motivations. This process and graphic layout keep it clear. For example . . .

(Blue) GOAL: What you want to accomplish

> **(Red)** What's involved, Who, When (timing: start or completion) or how (if you know).

>> **(Green)** Who benefits from the goal accomplishment.

>>> **(Purple)** How you'll feel when you accomplish it!

I use blue for the goal, red for the details of accomplishing it, green for who benefits, and purple for how I'll feel when it's accomplished. If these are your color choices, you will keep adding goals, what's involved, who benefits and how you'll feel when accomplished in each color per answer—all goals in blue, what's involved in red, etc. The three questions beneath each goal reinforce the "WHY." They are important and will serve as fuel for you and your success.

These are examples of carefully created vision boards . . .

(For more information about creating your vision board, go to RickHale.com for examples and links to video tutorials.)

YOU'VE DONE IT!

At this point, you've looked into the future to determine what you want your five-year-future self to look like. You've cast the vision and dared to dream. You've thought through your goals and intentions. Your vision board is a collection of those crystallized, urgent priorities in all areas of your life, succinctly summarized in one place. By writing out your goals and intentions and writing down what is most important on your vision board, you are using the written word to your advantage. You are scripting your own future self—not what anyone else wants for you. You now have a plan to achieve that ideal five-year-future self that started as only a theoretical concept and then became a hopeful vision.

Place your vision board in a location where you can see it every day. Many choose to hang it in their office so it's a constant reminder of their goals and priorities. Mine is in my closet where I can start each day reminding myself of my dreams, goals, and motivations. Seeing them the at the beginning of each day puts my subconscious mind to work. It also prepares me to throw my energy into doing what I can each day to make them happen. In addition, I ask God for the wisdom and courage to make decisions that lead to my becoming a better person (an area where I'm convinced my vision always aligns with His). Wisdom without the courage to act is like a racecar without gas. It looks cool, but it's going nowhere.

Of course, as you progress toward your intentions over several years, some of your specific goals are likely to change. It's common to adjust your goals as your situation changes, especially when you're considering so many different categories of life. As long as you remain on the path to fulfilling your intentions, you'll come out ahead. The only lasting goal, in my humble opinion, is to have quality relationships and experiences that are motivated by your most cherished intentions.

THE HAPPINESS FACTOR

I suspect some of you just finished doing a lot of work to create your vision board, and you've suddenly realized I'm promising you a payoff five years from now. That sounds a lot like a con game, doesn't it?

I do believe the most significant result of your vision board will be the much more satisfying life you create for yourself . . . eventually. However, I'm also convinced you'll see other results much sooner. As you pursue your distinct goals to achieve a richer, fuller life, you will begin to notice an increase in happiness as you get closer. Some people believe that happiness is the result of becoming wildly successful. It's just the opposite. Happiness is generated during the journey toward your destination as you overcome challenges, clear hurdles, interact with new and creative people you meet, and begin to see how regular growth is making you a more persistent and positive individual.

This observation should come as no surprise. It aligns with our previous explanation of the RAS (reticular activation system) in your brain that can be prompted to come up with positive answers to properly posed mental puzzles.

I recommend a book by Harvard professor Shawn Achor, *The Happiness Advantage*. He describes how we keep looking for some degree of success that will trigger happiness in our lives: a raise, promotion, weight loss, or whatever. Yet whatever degree of happiness comes from that event then leaves just as quickly. He explains:

> With each victory, our goalposts of success keep getting pushed further and further out, so that happiness gets pushed over the horizon.

> Even more important, the formula is broken because it is backward. More than a decade of groundbreaking research in

the fields of positive psychology and neuroscience has proven in no uncertain terms that the relationship between success and happiness works the other way around. Thanks to this cutting-edge science, we now know that happiness is the precursor to success, not merely the result. And that happiness and optimism actually *fuel* performance and achievement—giving us the competitive edge that I call the Happiness Advantage.

Waiting to be happy limits our brain's potential for success, whereas cultivating positive brains makes us more motivated, efficient, resilient, creative, and productive, which drives performance upward. This discovery has been confirmed by thousands of scientific studies and in my own work and research on 1,500 Harvard students and dozens of Fortune 500 companies worldwide.[5]

I've come to believe that happiness occurs when purpose and passion align and the result leads you to significance. It doesn't take a major success to create happiness. If I see I'm making consistent progress to live up to my potential, fulfill my purpose, and help make the world a better place, then every little step in that direction becomes a source of happiness.

I've also discovered a strong connection between happiness and gratitude. I've always believed that gratitude can be a powerful weapon against negative situations and pessimistic people, and a recent article from Harvard Medical School has confirmed it. The article explains that as someone's gratitude acknowledges the goodness of life, it also triggers a realization that "the source of that goodness lies at least partially outside themselves. As a result, being grateful also helps people connect to something larger than themselves as individuals— whether to other people, nature, or a higher power."

The Harvard article continues with results from a several studies. In one, the participants were divided into three groups and asked to write a few sentences each week on an assigned topic. The first group was instructed to write about things they were grateful for each week. The second group wrote about everyday irritations. The third group was told to write about anything that affected them that week (with no emphasis on either positive or negative events). After ten weeks, the participants who wrote about gratitude were more optimistic and better satisfied with life. An unexpected benefit was that they also got more exercise and made fewer trips to the doctor than the other groups.

Another study was conducted by University of Pennsylvania psychologist Dr. Martin E. P. Seligman, who tested different psychological interventions on 411 people regarding their early memories. One week's assignment was to "write and personally deliver a letter of gratitude to someone who had never been properly thanked for his or her kindness." In response to this assignment, participants immediately showed a huge increase in happiness scores—more than for any other intervention. In addition, the benefits lasted for a month.

While most of the Harvard studies showed a similar positive result to expressing gratitude, there were exceptions. Middle-aged divorced women who kept gratitude journals were no more satisfied than others who didn't. Children and adolescents who wrote and delivered letters of appreciation to the positive influencers in their lives weren't personally affected. Such findings suggest that gratitude is associated with emotional maturity. [6]

But like most other things, if you want to be a more grateful person (and happier as a result), you get better at it with practice. Developing a habit of writing thank-you notes or emails is a common starting point for many people, but simply telling other people "thank you" and expressing appreciation for what they do for you is also effective. Some people keep gratitude journals. Many practice prayer and meditation. I like to keep a gratitude list on my nightstand and add three things to it daily. And when I'm thankful for specific individuals or things they have done to make my life better, I try to be sure to let them know.

You've just put a lot of effort into your vision board. While you're thinking about vision, before we move on to something else, be sure to pause and look around for the people and events that make your life better. It's easy to get caught up in our own struggles and stresses to the point where we don't appreciate the good things in life and what others are doing for us. When that happens, we need to expand our vision.

You now know what you want to see in your five-year-future self. But if you show a little more gratitude to others this week, those positive changes begin right away.

QUESTIONS TO CONSIDER:

1. What has been your experience with organizational vision statements? (Were they instrumental in steering the direction of the business, nonprofit, or church? Or were they neglected or irrelevant?)

   Take some time to craft your personal or family vision statement. If it doesn't grab you, keep working on it until it does.

   Then craft your mission statement, which will begin to include some specific goals.

   How can you ensure your vision board will continue to keep you focused on being your best possible five-year-future self?

2. How would you describe the difference between goals and intentions? Why is it important to have both? Which should come first?

3. Describe a time when you met an ambitious personal goal but didn't achieve the satisfaction you were anticipating. How do you explain the unexpected letdown?

4. As you considered your five-year-future self, how did you feel about dreaming big and becoming well-grounded in all the categories? Was that exciting for you, or do you find it difficult to project such confidence?

5. Are you confident of achieving all the goals you've listed on your vision board? Explain.

6. Where will you place your vision board where it can inspire you every day?

7. In light of the scientific evidence of the benefits of gratitude, how do you plan to elevate your daily plan for expression?

CHAPTER 6

BEYOND A DOUBT

Once your vision board is complete, you will feel a rush of pure joy and euphoria as you gaze upon the possibilities for your life. However, after many years of leading people through this process, I've noticed another feeling that follows the euphoria.

That feeling is doubt . . . worry . . . uncertainty. People start second-guessing themselves: "Can I really do this?" "Is this vision possible for me?" "Should I really go for it?"

Doubt can serve a useful purpose. In an article titled "Emotional Agility," the authors observe: "All healthy human beings have an inner stream of thoughts and feelings that include criticism, doubt, and fear. That's just our minds doing the job they were designed to do: trying to anticipate and solve problems and avoid potential pitfalls."

The problem is that we don't always handle those thoughts properly, either responding as if they are gospel truth or going to the other extreme and attempting to rationalize them away. The authors add:

Effective leaders don't buy into *or* try to suppress their inner experiences. Instead they approach them in a mindful, values-driven, and productive way—developing what we call *emotional agility*. In our complex, fast-changing knowledge economy, this ability to manage one's thoughts and feelings is essential to business success.[7]

Your limiting beliefs threaten to creep in and hold you back from living the life of your dreams. They are your first obstacle to overcome. It is imperative that you go on the offensive, preparing yourself to stay focused and keep moving forward rather than being held back by feelings of self-doubt.

Your limiting beliefs, if you do not handle them correctly, can be like handcuffs, shackling you to a lesser life than what is available to you! You can prevent much confusion and despair if you avoid the handcuffs before you even put them on.

IT'S TIME TO CRUSH IT!

I recommend a goal-setting process adapted from Gary Keller at Keller Williams. You'll find helpful resources in his book, *The One Thing*, coupled with on-line resources. I also like a proven approach of a goal-setting tool called "Crush It 1-3-5." I like it because this method helps you crush (obliterate) your limiting beliefs in order to crush (excel at) your biggest goals! The process helps convince your brain to believe your own story by creating an evidential path to success.

Your vision board shows your end goals, but first you must pave the way to each individual goal. Just setting the goal and thinking positive thoughts are not enough. If you are going to be the first person in your family to go to college, for example, you likely have years of negative programming to overcome. You've never personally witnessed the path to a college degree. You may have never been told you can do it. This is an obstacle, a rock in the road. You need to create a mental path where none existed before. (If one already existed, you would already have accomplished that goal.)

Try it for yourself. First, select *one* of your big goals from your vision board. This is the "1" in "Crush It 1-3-5." Write down that one big goal at the top of a piece of paper or new computer document. Under the one big goal, list *three* strategies you could implement to accomplish that goal. For example, if your big goal is to lose twenty pounds, then the three strategies might include:

1. Train for a 5k (or longer, depending on your goals);

2. Eat a healthy diet; and

3. Reduce daily stress.

All three of these strategies will help you accomplish your big goal.

Finally, under each of your three strategies, list *five* small, manageable tasks you can complete to make progress toward that strategy. For example, if your strategy is to "Train for a 5k run," your five tasks might include:

1. Contact a local running club or running expert to get proper advice/coaching;

2. Purchase a reputable brand of running shoes;

3. Research online for tips and inspiration;

4. Purchase a running timer (to monitor running and walking intermittently until you build the muscle to run longer distances); and

5. Sign up for an upcoming 5k.

I'm using this method even now. I've gotten beyond 5ks, and I'm trying to increase my distances without trying to do too much too fast. Fortunately, I recently had the privilege of meeting Charlie Engle while I had my #1 task in mind. I was looking for reliable advice on running, and at an event I attended I was introduced to Charlie: an ultramarathon runner, expert on training and pushing your body, and the author of *Running Man*. I realized Charlie could help me get past my limiting beliefs because he had already done so. He has transformed himself from out of shape to tiptop shape, and he overcame some significant life challenges that had been created by substance abuse and addiction.

Charlie began with marathons, and he has run more than one marathon in a single day. When he wanted more of a challenge, he began to run ultramarathons, races that went for thirty-five, fifty, and sometimes hundreds of miles, racing in some of the most unforgiving places on earth. He even ran across the Sahara Desert—the only person to successfully accomplish that feat. (The heat at times actually melted his shoes.) The Matt Damon-produced documentary, *Running the Sahara*, followed Engle as he led a team on that harrowing, record-breaking, 4,500-mile run that helped raise millions of dollars for charity. The point of this story is that there are people with experiences and expertise that get great joy in helping you with your goals and mission.

It is important to create positive momentum before limiting beliefs take over. Charlie was my first call, and he agreed to show me the critical path to success before I allowed myself to sit around and wallow in doubt. He is helping me see my next tasks as possible. What a reliable resource and role model!

Here's another example. I'll show you how to chart the process if, say, you decide to attack the goal of learning to play the guitar. Your Crush It 1-3-5 table may look like this:

(You'll find a worksheet at the end of this chapter, and you can download a full-size version at RickHale.com.)

CRUSH IT!

1

Big Goal: Learn to play the guitar

3		
Find an instrument.	Find a teacher.	Find people to play/ jam with.

5		
1. Decide: guitar vs. bass? Acoustic vs. electric?	1. Ask other musicians for a referral.	1. Ask around at music stores.
2. Identify and compare music styles I like.	2. Inquire at local music stores.	2. Go to local shows and meet artists playing the style I prefer.
3. Get feedback from guitarists I know.	3. Google tips and sources.	3. Attend open mic nights at local venues.
4. Research prices.	4. Evaluate available online training.	4. Seek referrals via websites, Facebook, and peers.
5. Make the purchase.	5. Interview, choose the best option, and commit.	5. Market myself on websites for musicians' connections.

Now I have a plan! It's beginning to look like a realistic and attainable way to start meeting my goal.

But wait. I can feel those persistent limiting beliefs still hanging around. They've been silenced somewhat by my offensive attack on my big goal, but they haven't disappeared. It is time to put those pesky beliefs on paper and talk back to them.

I've found that most attempts fail not because the goal is too challenging, but rather that the person's fear is too great and stubborn obstacles block the path to success. Remove the obstacle and you'll open conscious pathways that allow your subconscious mind to navigate the situation.

This strategy was introduced to me by Bob Kilinski, a lifelong mentor and friend. He used the basic format of the regular 1-3-5 format first introduced to me by Gary Keller. Gary's focuses on the positive steps in goal-setting, but Bob called his complimentary approach "Renegade 1-3-5." Instead of simply scripting what you need to do to meet your goals, you also lean in and ask yourself, *What's keeping me from it?* I call it "Inhibitor 1-3-5."

The Renegade 1-3-5 is Bob's challenge to overcome fear that disables you by clarifying your big why (your life's purpose) in a paragraph, along with key milestones ("big rock" goals) required to move you toward that perfect life. You then document what inhibitors have kept you from reaching that milestone. In other words, instead of focusing on steps forward, you focus just as much on roadblocks and detours that have prevented you from making progress. Many of us set the same goals year after year, but we come up short and do it all again and again. Instead, Bob suggests identifying what causes the recurring derailment.

Then describe what it will take to overcome the barrier. For some of us, awareness of the limiting belief is a huge step. Then we can visualize an action-based path to overcome the debilitating element, pushing the fear aside. Fear of failure and rejection are powerful forces that can freeze progress. Clearly identifying the hindrance helps you take steps that are more focused on overcoming the real hindrances. You'll no longer be confused that you don't know why you can't make progress, and you'll no longer be frustrated that you're stuck in mediocrity. Now, each step forward increases momentum. Progress and not perfection is the key.

In the example below, I outlined the inhibitors that come to mind when I read through my task list. Not every task will necessarily have an inhibitor, but when one creeps in, make a plan and talk back to the limiting belief in a way that is concrete and believable.

INHIBITOR 1-3-5

1

Goal: Play the guitar

3 INHIBITORS

I don't know which guitar to buy.	Lessons are expensive.	I'm afraid I'll stink.

5 POSSIBLE SOLUTIONS

1. Talk to a friend who plays well.	1. Save before signing up.	1. Get feedback from friends.
2. Consult with a salesman.	2. Ask friends for advice.	2. Ask instructor for more help.
3. Think about an upgrade now.	3. Ask for a trial lesson.	3. Find your niche.
4. Try several.	4. Consider a group lesson.	4. Remember to have fun.
5. Consider the options.	5. Ask for lessons as presents.	5. Celebrate small wins.

The Crush It and the Inhibitor 1-3-5 exercises should help you think through what is needed in specific circumstances and help you keep moving forward. However, if you continue to be derailed in your progress by persistent self-doubt, you might need to start by addressing that issue more directly. Books and articles abound on the widespread problem of self-doubt, its causes, and how to confront and overcome it. An article in *Inc.* called it "probably the most powerful limiting force in your life. Left unchecked, it can define who you are and determine what you're able to do."[8]

Sources agree that self-doubt is quite common. It's not just an affliction among unsure people trying to muster the courage to try something new, like running your first 5k or joining a band. At some point, we've all been there. Even many writers and artists with long histories of accomplishment find themselves, with each new project, doubting if they can replicate their success. So while there's no shame in self-doubt, that doesn't mean we should ignore it. William Shakespeare wrote, "Our doubts are traitors, and makes us lose the good we oft might win by fearing to attempt."

The key is to learn to see self-doubt as just another hurdle we need to clear, not a wall that stops us in our tracks. Ignoring it won't make it go away. Common advice for dealing with self-doubt includes trying to identify the source of your feelings (for many, it starts in childhood), becoming aware of patterns and triggers, increasing positive self-talk, and putting an end to (or minimizing) your tendency to compare yourself to other people. And since many of these suggestions are easier said than done, almost everyone recommends you find someone to use as a sounding board about your self-doubt. If you have wise and understanding friends, they may be able to offer all the help you need. If not, or if your self-doubt is more deeply rooted than most, a professional therapist can be a great help.

Use logic and good judgment. Realize that everyone goes through what you're going through at times. Yet if you just can't seem to shake it, or if your goals are repeatedly being short-circuited, your self-doubt is likely more severe than most. Believe me, your life will get much better as soon as doubt is no longer a permanent mindset and becomes only an occasional hindrance as you continue your journey to success and fulfillment.

CATCH A VISION OF YOUR NEW DESTINATION

You've just put a lot of effort into creating your vision board. By now you should be looking at a list of challenging but reasonable goals you'd like to accomplish in the next five years. You even have a method to help you overcome self-doubt as you being to wonder how in the world you'll ever be able to do all those things. Yet still, you may feel overwhelmed at times. If so, let me give you some examples of how I've seen this method work in the past.

I've taken countless groups and individuals through this process, and it's always exciting to see how it changes the course of someone's life. One of the first was Darcy, a young woman I hired to be on my sales team. At the time, she was renting an apartment and was single. Her goals were very different from mine, given her youth and unique life experiences. She recognized that the area where she wanted to see the most growth was in her personal life. Consequently, her vision board included a lot of goals about developing a rich family life. She wanted a spouse, a home, a new SUV, and children to fill up seats in it!

Darcy didn't know how she would get there, but she knew what she wanted and never lost sight of that future self she saw in her mind. She constantly worked toward her dreams with heightened awareness for clues that looked like the vision she cast for herself and her new family. During the next five years, I saw Darcy's entire world change as she fulfilled many of her dreams.

As you begin to go through your own vision board process, don't get hung up on *how* you'll accomplish your goals. Don't worry about how you'll meet that spouse or have those kids. Don't worry about how you'll get those clients or realign your business. "How" is the wrong question at this stage. Instead, I urge you to focus on "why."

You may remember that when I shared goals from my own vision board in the previous chapter, one of them was, "Help children in poverty in inner-city Atlanta." Let me tell you how that became one of my priorities and how I saw it accomplished.

One day, before I discovered the power of the future self exercise, I had an experience that changed my life. I was on my way to see a foreclosed and abandoned property in an economically challenged section of Atlanta. On the way, I saw two young kids playing in a puddle in the middle of the street after a rain. As I got closer I could see they couldn't be more than two or three years old, so I stopped the car and waited for an adult to come out and rescue them. I waited for what felt like an hour, although it was probably closer to ten minutes.

While I waited, I looked around for someone who should have been supervising them. The only adult I could see was an older lady a few houses down, passed out on the front porch with a bottle covered in a paper sack. I tapped the horn as delicately as possible not to alarm the kids and thankfully she jolted awake and realized where her kids (or grandkids were) and re-engaged, but in a stupor. I peered around the corner and saw what looked to me like a group of prostitutes and drug dealers, not abnormal for this particular inner-city neighborhood.

But no one was watching those kids. No one. I sat there and asked myself, *Who are the role models for these two children? Three square meals? Tucked in every night safely with a couple of fun kid books read to them? Where will they be in ten years? Twenty years? How do they "flip the script" on their circumstances and create a brighter future?*

The plight of those two kids stayed with me. Even to this day, I want to drive back to that puddle, put them in my car, and take care of them. So when I was going through my Future Self process, I wrote that I wanted to do something philanthropic for the poorest kids in Atlanta. I didn't know what I could possibly do, but the thought of those kids drove me. I had no idea *how*, but my *why* was very strong. I remembered from my childhood that a few positive, encouraging voices at the right moments injected a sense of security and changed the trajectory of my life.

Joey Russo is a friend who works with college students at Kennesaw State University. He recently told me about one of the concepts the university teaches at its Entrepreneurial School. As soon as a student comes to a decision and chooses a path for a career or entrepreneurial endeavor, the opportunities expand almost instantly. Once that first big decision is made, new doors usually present themselves and often open with little effort, when prior to the decision to shift direction, those doors weren't even visible.

Another wise friend, Steve Kout, has a lot of experience with mission, vision, and values creation. We've had spirited debates around the importance of first steps in decision-making. I'd always held out that it was essential to have at least an inkling of how a distant goal might be accomplished to keep oneself on course, but Steve's assertion is that simply scripting it is enough to hit the go button. He has just about convinced me. If you're driving to California from Georgia at night, you certainly don't see your goal. Your headlights illuminate only fifty yards or so at a time, and that's sufficient. The key is getting the car started and pointed in the right direction. Then, along the way you can modify direction, make appropriate turns, and adjust accordingly as you need to.

If you wait to know exactly how you'll achieve your goal or who will help you, you'll be holding yourself back. How do I know? Because I was four years and eleven months into my five-year vision and still hadn't met my goal to help inner-city children in Atlanta when I met Dave and heard about Camp Grace. To be perfectly honest, I'd crushed almost every goal in every goal category, except the one focused on helping at-risk children. My prayer was the same every day: "Dear God, please show me the way, and grant me the wisdom and the courage to act on it when it shows up in my life." A month before the five-year mark, I began to doubt a bit. Was it me? Was I supposed to be more proactive and pursue the charity or agency to fulfill the goal and complete a fantastic five-year run? Was God really listening to me at that point? And then . . . it happened!

CAMP GRACE

One day I got a call from a guy named Dave. He simply said, "Hi, I'm Dave Pridemore, and I'm working on a project to serve underserved youth in our city. Many of them live in the shadows of the buildings you work in. I'm not calling with an ask. I just want a few minutes of your time to share my dream and see if you know someone who might find it interesting." I loved the non-ask approach and gladly took the meeting. It sounded interesting, but truthfully, in that moment I didn't connect the dots to my vision board (hard to believe, right?) because I was really busy and got calls all the time from people who wanted to meet with me.

Dave and I met a few days later in a conference room in my office, and he started to share his story and his dream. Within ten minutes, I began to tear up and feel an emotional tidal wave inside me—I realized *his dream* was directly tied to *my dream*! He talked about providing a safe environment and lasting relationships for at-risk kids—and ultimately, give them hope and inspiration! As I was overcome with emotion, he stared at me in disbelief. Then I explained my vision board. He is a man of amazing faith, and he immediately understood what God had done in that brief conversation. He gave God the credit for everything, including our new friendship, regardless of the outcome. The *what* was a result of the *who* I'd met. Dave was the open door to align my goals with his organization. It's an honor to connect with people who care so deeply and make such a difference in the lives of often-overlooked children.

Popular radio host Paul Harvey often invited people to share heartwarming stories, but he always asked them to tell the backstory that made it even more amazing. It was "and now, the rest of the story." Here's the rest of the story about Dave Pridemore. He's a pastor in Atlanta who had retired from corporate America to pursue his vision for helping the poorest of the poor in Atlanta. He was in the process of creating a camp experience called Camp Grace where he planned to bring poor kids from the inner city for a whole week of swimming, playing, riding horses, and hearing about God's love for them. He had even formulated a plan for staying connected with the kids and mentoring them throughout the year so the course of their lives could truly be changed. At the time, he was renting a camp in northern Georgia for a few weeks to learn what was involved with running it.

Dave told me he envisioned a top-quality camp, yet one that would cost essentially nothing for the underprivileged kids who attended. He was looking for partners to help him build cabins on his camp. He said that he could build a cabin for $25,000. I knew what he was doing was a game changer for many and I couldn't wait to learn more about it and engage!

Truthfully, I was thinking even bigger than just me and my potential to be a part of the big plan. I thought it would be a magic moment for

Dave if I could compel my colleagues at Keller Williams to give it a look and maybe buy into his vision as well. On the way home I called Kay, my regional leader, and asked for five minutes to share the vision for Camp Grace at our leadership meeting the next day. I must admit that it didn't feel very magical when she gave me an emphatic "no." Those that know me are well aware I don't take "no" very well if I believe in something. So I stated my case again to be absolutely sure "no" really meant "no," but I got nowhere. Kay admitted that the idea sounded good and that we might be able to help at some point, but she also made clear that it was corporate policy that no one can bring personal agendas or charities to the business meetings in our region.

Poof. There went the magic. Our meeting the next day was long and a bit mundane, and by midafternoon my thoughts had turned to what I wasn't getting done in my office while I was sitting there. Kay was speaking about monitoring our budgets when she suddenly went into a coughing fit. What happened next was one of the most miraculous things I have ever been a part of. Between coughs, while she was recovering, Kay said, "Hey, Rick, tell everyone about Camp Grace."

Caught off-guard and totally unprepared after the firm "no" I had received the day before, I made an impromptu but passionate presentation of Dave's vision for supporting the poorest of the poor in our community. When I told my peers about Camp Grace, they didn't just smile and nod. They caught the vision that day, agreeing to meet Dave and present his plans to their respective real estate offices. Not long afterward, Kay Evans and her partner, Bob Kilinski, each funded a cabin on their own, demonstrating amazing generosity. They also shared the vision at a later leadership meeting in Austin where another friend, Bev Steiner, donated a cabin on the spot! Mo Anderson, our CEO, also funded a cabin, sight unseen, knowing that Kay and Bob would only tell him about a charitable investment that had real value to them. When these people learned how they could have a direct impact on the lives of less fortunate children, they were all in!

As a group, the thirty Keller Williams Georgia offices raised almost half a million dollars to build almost twenty cabins—enough for 300 kids. The cabins are all connected and have been dubbed "Fort KW," and there the poorest of the poor in Atlanta can enjoy a summer camp that rivals the best camps in America! It's stories like these that remind me why I love my job at the organization Forbes recently voted the happiest company in America to work for. The people there go beyond training and coaching; their collective generous spirit and commitment to one another and the communities they serve ignites joy and a sense of purpose.

I am thrilled to report that Camp Grace continues to expand and is turning into one of the most successful and life-changing ministries to urban youth in cities throughout the southeast. Dave and I are partners in ministry, and I could have easily missed this opportunity if I hadn't gone through the vision boarding process.

The first lesson I learned from this experience was confirmation about the need to avoid obsessing on the "how" and pay more attention to the "why" on my vision board goals.

The second lesson was that vision isn't only about me, and not even up to me alone. I didn't have half a million dollars of my own to help Dave out, but the united commitment of a strong, caring community did.

If a vision is compelling enough, it will attract others who are eager to help improve the lives of people in need. The real answer was attached to "who." Who needed to know about Camp Grace that might engage in this amazing journey and outcome? (Visit www. thecampgrace.com for more information.) Similarly, who can also be an advocate, coach or consultant who knows the ins and outs of success in the area of your big goal?

And the third lesson, one that has really stayed with me, is the value of dreaming *big*. I've come to believe that if some or most of my plans don't scare the heck out of me, they might be too small. When I choose to share them with a friend, I expect to see a reaction that indicates, "You're crazy!"

WHAT IF . . .?

One final lesson: When you start challenging yourself with musings that begin with "What if . . . ?" be careful how you finish those questions. If doubt and fear have set in, you'll find yourself wondering:

- What if I'm not as capable as I think to meet this goal?
- What if I don't get the funding?
- What if the economy tanks after I get started?
- What if . . . (fill in your favorite fear/excuse here)?

Those kinds of what-if questions have wrecked untold thousands of brilliant plans, amazing ideas, and world-changing opportunities. If you start to reconsider some of your well-conceived and potentially beneficial plans, take the advice that's frequently circulated these days: Be afraid, but do it anyway.

One key to getting beyond your doubts and fears is to edit your what-if questions. Rewrite the endings to transform them into motivational and affirming possibilities. Bold, positive plans start by considering:

- What if anything were possible?
- What if the entire universe was on my side?
- What if I were guaranteed success in my endeavors?

In addition, remember that you probably won't need to accomplish every big goal on your vision board singlehandedly. Dream big, make good plans, and remain open to finding allies who are almost as excited about your ideas as you are. When you succeed, it just makes the celebration that much bigger!

Remember that it's not always just your private dream—others will want to join you. You may be the spark that lights the fire, or you may be an additional log on an already burning blaze. And the light and heat you provide may draw others into the big dream, big goals, and big impact.

If your dream seems too big, don't be intimidated. The *what* and the *how* may be daunting, but perhaps you'll find a *who* that opens doors for you like Dave did for me. I didn't know how to build and run a summer camp, but Dave did, and I was thrilled to join his team. When your dream seems bogged down, don't give up. Look for open doors, and when you find one, walk through it. You may need to walk through several, but you'll find the right one sooner or later. When it happens, you'll realize the process taught you valuable lessons you can use for the rest of your life . . . and you'll make even more of an impact wherever you go.

QUESTIONS TO CONSIDER:

1. On a scale of 1 (not at all) to 10 (overwhelmingly), to what extent are you plagued by self-doubt when facing a daunting task? Why do you think your number isn't lower?

2. What are some projects or activities you would have tried by now if you were assured you couldn't fail? Why does the possibility of failure prevent you from attempting them?

3. Choose one of the goals from your vision board that creates a lot of uncertainty when you think about it, and go through the Crush It 1-3-5 exercise. (To download a PDF go to RickHale.com.)

1

Big Goal: _____

---

3 CRUCIAL STEPS

Step 1:

Step 2:

Step 3:

---

5 ACTION POINTS FOR EACH STEP:
(HOW, WHAT OR WHO?)

Step 1:

Action 1:

Action 2:

Action 3:

Action 4:

Action 5:

Step 2:

Action 1:

Action 2:

Action 3:

Action 4:

Action 5:

Step 3:

Action 1:

Action 2:

Action 3:

Action 4:

Action 5:

4. Now, using the one big goal and the three crucial steps, use the following chart to work on your Inhibitor 1-3-5 exercise to overcome obstacles. (To download a PDF go to RickHale.com.)

1

Big Goal: _____

3 INHIBITORS

Step 1:

Step 2:

Step 3:

5 POSSIBLE SOLUTIONS

Step 1:

Action 1:

Action 2:

Action 3:

Action 4:

Action 5:

Step 2:

Action 1:

Action 2:

Action 3:

Action 4:

Action 5:

Step 3:

Action 1:

Action 2:

Action 3:

Action 4:

Action 5:

CHAPTER 7

FIRST THINGS FIRST

Within a few years of beginning my entrepreneurial career in real estate sales, I was selling approximately one hundred houses per year and even on the cusp of opening my first Keller-Williams Realty franchised office. In my determination to outwork everyone else, I had done quite well my first year in terms of income, and only a few years later I was making ten times that much, annually. Life in the career lane was good.

I boasted to clients that I was the guy they could call day or night— that's how committed I was to their success. And they did. I was the realtor who could talk them off a metaphorical ledge if they were understandably stressed-out over buying and selling a home. Many days I would speed home from work after 7 P.M. just to clock in before my two-year-old Alex went to bed. Like so many other busy executives, I always told everyone that family came first. I might have actually believed it.

Then, one evening I was at home, but still working. I was pacing around our kitchen island, cellphone in hand, attending to the latest concern of one of my clients, when I noticed Alex had toddled into the kitchen. Do you know what he was doing? He was pacing around the kitchen island behind me, with his hand on his ear, pretending to have a conversation.

I told my client, "I'll have to call you back tomorrow morning."

That was a real Cat's-in-the-Cradle moment for me. I've always believed that circumstances and honest people will show you where you are making mistakes, but it's up to you to receive the message and make the appropriate change. Well, I got the message that day. That image of Alex holding his "phone" to his ear is still burned into my mind. From that moment, I began setting real boundaries.

THE POWER OF BOUNDARIES

In their book, *Boundaries*, Henry Cloud and John Townsend write:

Boundaries define us. They define *what is me* and *what is not me*. A boundary shows me where I end and someone else begins, leading me to a sense of ownership.

Knowing what I am to own and take responsibility for gives me freedom. If I know where my yard begins and ends, I am free to do with it what I like. Taking responsibility for my life opens up many different options. However, if I do not "own" my life, my choices and options become very limited.[9]

I couldn't live with the consequences of a child who thought his daddy would rather work than spend quality time with him. I had to take responsibility for having allowed clients, work, and other worthwhile pursuits to crowd out my *most important* pursuits. I made the decision, right there in the kitchen, to change my boundary lines.

I wish I could tell you that the moment I made the decision, everything immediately became easier and better, but I can't. The truth is, it takes time to set up boundaries after years of allowing anyone and everyone to hijack your time. I'd say that it took almost two years

FIRST THINGS FIRST | 149

before I had established a regular routine that consistently allowed me to give my family the time and attention they deserved.

It started with simply changing my voicemail. I let friends and clients know that if they had tried to reach me after 7 p.m., I would call them back in the morning. I also had to hire new people. I determined not to work on Sundays, even though Sundays are often a lucrative workday for a real estate agent. But Sundays are also a critical day for family interaction, and a time to connect with God and spiritual energy. I decided I needed to set an example for my children that God and family are more important than work—no easy task for a self-professed workaholic. A few years later, once my team was in place, I stopped taking appointments on Saturdays. At that point, we had the ability to serve clients seven days a week, and I was free of guilt in a field where timeliness and availability reign supreme!

I soon learned that setting boundaries needed to include technology. Many of us become so attached to our cellphones that they become an extension of our arms. Even now, my wife understands my commitment to being responsive to the needs of my employees, coworkers, and friends, yet we've both realized that my round-the-clock availability was eroding our connectivity and intimacy. In addition to reducing my "availability hours" at work, we've also started leaving all phones and screens behind when enjoying family time. It's made a tremendous difference in the quality of our conversations. (I encourage her to remind me when I'm mentally drifting and not really present, which again, isn't easy for an A-type go-getter that's also a people pleaser!)

I like the advice that a lot of speakers and coaches are using these days: "Be where your feet are." Instead of busily rushing around and preparing for the next item on your to-do list, stop and take time to be present right where you are, with whomever you are with, paying full attention to what is transpiring at that moment. I've discovered that conversations, meetings, and other personal interactions become so much more effective (and rewarding) if my mind is in the same general vicinity as my feet! Technology is one of many distractions that can derail our thoughts and highjack moments meant to be shared face-to-face.

A TWENTY PERCENT TIP . . .
TO HELP ESTABLISH PRIORITIES

Back at around the dawn of the twentieth century, Vilfredo Pareto, an Italian economist, discovered an interesting connection between input and output in various settings. The observation that started his thinking was that twenty percent of the pea plants in his garden produced eighty percent of the pea pods. As he started examining other areas for similar uneven distribution, he found in agriculture that eighty percent of the land in Italy was owned by twenty percent of the population. In business, eighty percent of production came from twenty percent of the companies.

In time, the Pareto Principle, also known as the 80/20 rule, became a standard formula that was adopted for widespread application in business and other interests. The exact percentages vary a bit, of course, but it's a fair estimate to figure that twenty percent of a company's salespeople generate eighty percent of business; twenty percent of hospital patients account for eighty percent of healthcare spending; eighty percent of your personal time is spent with twenty percent of your friends and family; and so forth.[10]

I AM AMAZED BY THE NUMBER OF PEOPLE WHO KNOW THE
DEFINITION OF THE 80/20 RULE,
AND YET THEY DON'T APPLY IT TO THEIR OWN LIVES.

I believe it stands to reason that twenty percent of your weekly activity results in eighty percent of your happiness, satisfaction, and wealth. In order to draw boundary lines in the right place and guarantee time for your top priorities, it is crucial to identify what is the most critical twenty percent of your life, business, family, and health.

For example, in business I help other realtors identify their twenty percent: generating listings, responding to calls, negotiating contracts, and going to closings. The other eighty percent, such as data entry, sending out newsletters, and posting on social media can be done by a college intern or marketing professional. And I remind them what Brian Tracy wrote in *Eat That Frog*, "One of the very worst uses of time is to do something very well that need not be done at all."[11]

As for my personal time, I haven't mowed my lawn in twenty years. Why? Because instead I try to block off those sunny southern afternoons for boating with my wife and kids at the lake or attending Georgia football games! Yardwork isn't part of my critical twenty percent, so I don't do it.

Have you ever taken the time to ponder what you're worth per hour? I have, and I found it to be an interesting exercise. Do it now! Write on a sheet of paper or in the margin of this book the amount you believe is your hourly value. If you have a salaried, fixed-pay job, it's easy. Just take the number of hours invested at work per pay period, and divide into the salary paid by your employer. If you're a business owner, salesperson, or someone who receives productivity-based compensation, your income probably fluctuates. Even so, calculate your hours worked over a certain period and the income you generated by those hours. That will tell you exactly what you're worth per hour for the reporting period. Now, consider what you did to achieve that return on invested time, and ponder ways to do fewer low-paying tasks and more high-paying activities to elevate your hourly pay. And remember, there's no job too small (or too large, for that matter) to outsource or subcontract if it costs less than your optimal pay for a particular activity.

You can't draw effective boundary lines until you first identify what's most important to you. That's why I had you spend the previous few chapters identifying the categories that matter to you, seeing what you want your five-year-future self to look like, and then writing specific goals and intentions to help you get there. You should already have a clear idea of what you most want to accomplish. Now you just need to put up blockades to prevent unimportant tasks from hijacking those truly critical priorities.

In his book, *The One Thing*, Gary Keller opens with a Russian proverb: "If you chase two rabbits, you will not catch either one." He recommends creating a space where you can focus on your "one thing"—your most important work priority. This is your "bunker," a place to go where you have blocked off uninterrupted time and have everything you need to work. In your bunker you can write your book, call potential leads, or work on your critical goal.[12] I encourage you to build a specific bunker for every goal you have deemed important. Create a safe place where no one can interrupt or pull you off track, even though it may not be easy to do so. Like I said, it took me about two years just to build my family sanctuary. I had to retrain staff, hire new people, revise messages, change the culture of my office, and set new standards. But in the end, it was surely worth it.

THE MAGIC OF A DAY PLANNER

It may not exactly be magic, but a day planner is an extraordinarily helpful tool. Yes, I know, some of us are naturally gifted in planning, and others . . . not so much. I don't need to encourage the first group to keep a daily planner, but I want to focus on those who are more spontaneous and shoot from the hip. A day planner—whether a physical notebook or app on your phone or other device—keeps you focused on what you need to do that day. It reinforces your BIG GOALS. It injects gas into your passionate intentions so you stay on track with how you want your life to count. Let me offer a few suggestions:

1. Refresh your plans each week and each day. Each week, write down the four or five most important five-year goals, and each day, write down the specific activities that will take you a step or two closer to those goals.

2. Find a friend and encourage each other. You don't need to go over every detail of your day, but it will help a lot to ask, "What's important on your schedule today?" Avoid (as much as possible) people who are downers, and find time to spend with people who are optimistic. The greatest predictor of success is your social network. Don't take the status quo for granted. Move toward people who will have a positive influence on you.

3. Don't despise the redundancy. Yes, the goals will probably be the same week after week, but that's the point: you've set those five-year goals because they're imminently important to you! Writing them and reviewing them regularly reminds you what's most important and where you want to go.

4. As you use your day planner, your conscious and subconscious mind will help you identify opportunities and face challenges. Your reticular activator will be working double-time!

5. Keeping long-term goals top of mind is a crucial exercise. It reminds you why you get up and go to work every day, it inspires you to greatness, and it puts steel in your soul when

you face difficulties. People who refocus on the future every day are far more likely to get where they want to go.

This process is like checking your GPS as you ride down the highway. If you ignore it, you might be surprised by trouble you didn't expect. (In the next chapter, I'll share the "Day Planner Test"—an assessment you can perform to confirm your success living in the twenty percent.)

WRITE YOUR OWN STORY

When you look back on your life and consider the choices you made and how you spent your time, I believe you will say one of two things: either "I wish I had," or "I'm glad I did." What you need to realize as soon as possible is that it's your story, so the plot from now on is up to you. You can no longer edit your past, but you have the final authority to write all future chapters the way you want.

I've seen far too many people filled with regret when they realize they didn't live up to their potential, missed opportunities that were laid out before them, or settled for shallow relationships instead of making meaningful connections. Lots of those people had big dreams, valid plans, and high hopes . . . but they just didn't get there.

Since you have made it this far in the book, I know you are committed to your priorities. So far, you have defined them and described how to achieve them. But if you want to minimize your end-of-life regrets, you need to begin now to transfer all those wonderful hopes, dreams, and good intentions from your mind to your daily planner.

It has been said, "You always have time for the things you put first." The way to do that is to schedule those priorities. If you don't determine what is most important in your day-to-day life—and put it down on paper—others will decide for you. Your children are growing up whether you're spending sufficient time with them or not. Your wedding anniversary is going to roll around every year even if you've never followed through on that romantic getaway you promised years ago. Like so many other aspects of life, those things aren't going to change until you decide to change them.

When my children were six and four years old, I decided not to allow another year to go by without making plenty of memories. I was still insisting, "My family comes first," but if you peeked at my Day-Timer or opened my digital calendar, you would have seen a different story. So that year, I decided to spend six full weeks on vacation with the family. I didn't know how I was going to pull it off with the amount of work I had to do, but I trusted that everything else would fall in line.

First, I marked off a full week at Thanksgiving and a full week at Christmas, since most people aren't working then anyway, writing "Out of the Office" in my calendar. Next, I called a travel agent. (Surprisingly, they still exist today!) I said that I wanted to take four vacations, each for one week. I provided information about my kids' schedules, their likes and dislikes, and where we had traveled in the past. She went right to work, sending me ideas and travel plans. Within a week, we had scheduled four separate week-long vacations. There. Done. As soon as those six weeks of uninterrupted family time went into my schedule, my family *truly* became a priority.

Our schedules either confirm or betray our stated priorities. In business, I see leaders claim that their first priority is hiring the right people for each position, and yet they spend less than three hours with prospects before allowing them to join the team. And how many people do you know who are always talking about a desire for better health, but haven't seen the inside of a gym in months? If you plan to get in shape and yet leave your workout to chance, you'll never see the long-term change you wish to see in your physique and athletic ability. That's an easy fix: make an appointment with a physical trainer and prepay for three sessions each week for three months. Then, you can bet you won't miss that appointment.

At first, you may think you'll never be able to find the time and achieve all the goals on your vision board. But as you get better at prioritizing and scheduling, you may be surprised at how much more you'll accomplish.

You may have heard the story about the business professor who pulled out a clear jar and placed baseball-sized rocks in it, up to the top. He asked the class, "Is this pitcher full?" Many of them said yes. Then he pulled out a container of much smaller pebbles, poured them in, and they settled around the larger stones. Again he asked, "Is this full?" Some students were more reluctant to agree this time, but several nodded. The professor picked up a bag of sand and the class watched as the sand filled in all the empty spots in the jar. The professor asked, "*Now* is the jar full?" More confident, they all agreed that, indeed, nothing else could go into the jar. Finally, the professor pulled out a pitcher of water and poured a pint or so into the jar. He explained his point: "The rocks, pebbles, sand, and water are like your priorities, and the jar represents your time. If I had started with the sand and pebbles, I never could have fit in the larger rocks. But if you start with your biggest priorities and complete your tasks in proper order, you can do much more than you might think.

I'm naturally wired to be creative and spontaneous. If you're like me, structure is your greatest ally (even though you may sometimes see it as a foe). Tackle the highest priorities first and leave space to be creative. If you start with creativity first, you'll probably lose massive blocks of time. Your priorities should be reflected in your day planner every day. Trust me, I've learned the necessary formula for success is Structure = Freedom. If family is your priority, make sure your schedule reflects it. If you operate your business in a structured way, you'll have more margin for creativity and fun without suffering compromised results.

So remember: You write your own story. Clearly identify your priorities. Establish some boundaries. Determine how to focus more intently on your twenty percent, and carve out time in your schedule to do those things. If you do, your story will be a fascinating read, and you'll guarantee a happy ending.

QUESTIONS TO CONSIDER:

1. Have you set any boundaries to protect your personal/family life from your work obligations? If so, what inspired you to do so? And if not, did my story about Alex provide any motivation to convince you to avoid a similar personal regret?

2. Do a quick mental estimation of how much time you've spent on various projects this past week. Do you think you're investing eighty percent of your time into what your vision board suggests should be your top priorities? If not, what adjustments do you need to make?

3. Do you have a bunker? If not, where could you set it up, and how would you supply it to inspire and encourage you?

4. Look through the next several weeks in your daily calendar. Do your appointments reflect as much time spent on your top priorities as you wish? Do they reflect the dollars per hour you want them to?

5. Do you need to rearrange your schedule to accomplish more within your "jar" of available time? If so, how?

CHAPTER 8

MAKE THE MOST
OF EVERY DAY

Let's say you want to lose fifteen pounds. You're determined this time! You dust off your scale and start a journal to faithfully record your weight every day. You rejoice in every lost pound, yet soon find yourself more frequently bewailing the return of a half-pound here and quarter-pound there. For many people, the daily trip to the scale eventually becomes a dreaded moment. What gives? It's a wise and reasonable goal, and you've seen progress. Yet as far too many of us know, we find ourselves giving up before that goal is accomplished.

The problem is that we measure the wrong things. To make regular progress over the long term, we must learn to distinguish between *leading* indicators and *lagging* indicators. Weight loss is a lagging indicator. By the time you step on the scale, it is too late to change anything! You must start to measure your success based on leading indicators, such as:

- How many glasses of water did I drink today?
- How many minutes did I devote to cardiovascular exercise?
- How much of today's diet was high-fiber vegetables and fruit?
- How many hours of sleep did I get last night?
- How much time did I spend building muscle?

If you are only measuring lagging indicators, such as pounds lost, inches lost, or muscle gained, you are focusing too far in the future. You must begin with leading indicators.

SCOREKEEPING

This is not only true for health goals; it applies to every category of life. Distinguishing leading indicators from lagging indicators, and shifting your emphasis from the latter to the former, is crucial for success in business. Stephen Covey identifies four important disciplines needed to move into the world of high performance, the second of which is to "Create a Compelling Scoreboard." Your scoreboard is how you track your progress after your goals have been narrowed down and prioritized. And of course, before they can be scored, they must be measurable. Covey explains:

> The people who are involved, who will be evaluated, need to participate in establishing a compelling performance scoreboard that reflects the criteria built into the mission, values and strategy of an organization so that they can continuously stay aligned with the process and be both responsible and accountable. They need to emotionally connect to it and own it. This is *also* true of individuals, teams, departments or any person who has responsibility to complete a task or handle a project Everyone should be involved in developing the Scoreboard, and then be accountable to it. [13]

Once a goal has been established and you have set up your life and bunker to serve you well, how do you determine if you are moving closer to that goal? It is critical to track or "score" your progress regularly.

This process of scoring has always been important in my business, and I'm still refining it after years.

The main mistake I've seen when coaching people in this area is their difficulty in distinguishing leading indicators from lagging indicators. When keeping a daily scoreboard, the focus must be on *leading* indicators.

In economics, a leading indicator is defined as "an economic factor that changes *before* the economy changes in trend." Leading indicators tend to be based on *input*, while lagging indicators measure *output*— what has already happened. And in sales, a leading indicator would be the number of calls you make to prospects every day. Leading indicators *predict* change, rather than measuring the change itself.

As we often hear in management seminars, "You must inspect what you expect." In other words, pay close attention to the goals you expect to achieve. However, most people inspect the wrong things. Their scoreboard is not set up well, and their measurements aren't always accurate. Without the right scoreboard, most people give up, forget about their goals, or fall prey to discouragement.

What makes this task so challenging is that each goal needs to be measured, and often the leading indicators are not straightforward. It takes time to discover which indicators best predict future success. When you run into that problem, I suggest meeting with people who have already accomplished what you are trying to do.

With every goal on your vision board, try asking "Who?" instead of "How?"

Who has the answer? Who has already targeted the leading indicators for success in the categories that mean most to you? Most of my success has come from people, not events or products. I would not be where I am without people who were willing to share their expertise or perspective.

Pull out your vision board and review all your challenging goals. For each one, think of someone whom you believe has already discovered critical leading indicators and can be of help, and write down the name. Make a list and then set up meetings with those people. Ask them to describe the inputs they use to monitor progress toward that goal and how they measure success.

In some areas, the people who have found the right formula may be friends, neighbors, or colleagues. In other cases, you may not know anyone personally and will need to go outside your network to professional financial advisors, health coaches, life coaches, personal trainers, or authors.

Since your vision board is a collection of goals gleaned from twelve different categories, you aren't likely to find one person to provide the best advice in all those areas. In fact, you may not know *anyone* to turn to for help in certain categories. If that's the case, you'll probably need to make some new friends.

If no one in your life is any more financially astute than you are, then it is your mission to find someone who is. If no one in your life leads a healthy lifestyle, you may need to make some friends at your gym who will show you what works for them, search for a personal fitness trainer, or Google nutritionists online. You might even ask for a referral from your doctor. If you cannot quickly name anyone in your circle who has a good relationship with their children, then you should look around at your church, synagogue, or your child's next soccer game for parents who inspire you by the love they show their kids. Success leaves clues, and if you pay close attention, you'll find good role models. The person may not be your primary source of help, but he or she may be able to make a referral or recommend a book. Get to know people who can help with each of your vision board goals. Otherwise, you'll always be limited to what you already know. Again, let me remind you: what got you *here* won't get you *there*!

What is the difference between an average performer and a spectacular one? Twenty years ago, I would have said that some people were ultra-successful because they had a significant advantage in intellect, talent, charisma, or financial standing. However, since then I've learned that in most businesses, the difference between average and spectacular is smaller than you think.

In baseball, the difference can be one more hit per game, or even one more per week. In real estate, the difference is only one or two additional transactions per month. That little bit of extra effort or performance—done day after day or week after week—sets apart the stellar performers from the rest of the herd even netting as much as $120,000 or more in additional annual income.

Although the differences may be small, it's no simple matter to identify *which* small improvements will best bridge that gap. Knowledge is powerful when applied appropriately. Doing less, but doing the right things well, makes the difference. That's why Gary Keller's advice to discover "the one thing" in your situation will set you far ahead of others in your industry who spread their efforts and resources over numerous lesser pursuits.

WRITE ON!

Perfect days are the key to exemplary performance. Perfect days strung together effectively lead to perfect weeks, which of course create perfect months and an awesome year! Sounds too simple to be true, right? It's not. Perfect days are a sprint, and sprinting is far easier in terms of focus and results than tediously long marathons (months and years). My buddy Gene Rivers taught me many years ago that the war is won daily, not weekly or monthly, and certainly not with annual goals as the guide. We could paraphrase the point: "Win the day, win your life." It's not easy, but it's far less complicated than focusing on a month. Perfect days also help you create new habits, and they build confidence so you never settle.

When I'm training groups, I often ask them if they're "quitters." Frankly, it's a bit of a setup because we're all quitters from time to time—and some of us fairly often. Do you remember the concept of stopping one thing to exchange it for a higher priority? That's what I call "good quitting." But few achievers "wholesale quit" commitments, and they certainly don't think of themselves as quitters. However, you may think you're on task throughout the day, but if you find yourself easily distracted and multitasking (which is really task switching, which leads to disruption and inefficiency), you're still quitting. Leaving one commitment for another one, even for a short amount of time, is quitting, and it's probably depriving you of your highest and best outcome. You're actually "micro-quitting" a number of times each day and robbing yourself of focus, which impairs ultimate success. Of course, we're all good at justifying our distractions, but this habit takes you away from your twenty percent strength zone, your "one thing," and results in a lower return per hour.

The good news is that you may be only one small habit away from a quantum-leap improvement in your life and business. But how do you bridge that seemingly small gap and nail your *one* thing?

DAY PLANNER TEST

When I meet with young professionals who want to know how to move up the career ladder through improved performance, I always start by giving them a test. I call it "The Day Planner Test"—an exercise to reveal the overall effectiveness of their day, week, and month. Whether you keep your schedule electronically or with pen and paper, the exercise is the same. If you use a paper planner, you will need a yellow highlighter, red pen, and green highlighter. If you are using a digital planner, simply use the equivalent font colors to complete the exercise.

Open your planner to a single day. Go through that day and highlight in yellow everything that you did that was important, but not vital to your business. Once you have completed a day, continue through an entire week, and then an entire month, identifying those "yellow" tasks. In real estate, examples of items to highlight would include doing paperwork and data entry (other than writing a contract!), creating fliers, passive marketing, and installing yard signs—all low-level activities that do need to be done, yet don't result in highest return on investment. Once you have completed the yellow part, review your month and calculate the number of hours you spend on these important, yet non-vital tasks.

Next, with your red pen, go through a single day and mark through all your activities that had absolutely no impact on your business, reputation, or key goals. These could include meetings you didn't need to be part of, paperwork that could have been easily outsourced, or other periods of wasted time.

Finally, use your green highlighter to go through a single day and highlight everything you did where you were operating at highest efficiency—any activity critical to your success or the success of your clients. These activities are your top twenty percent, the crucial things to do to ensure you win the day! For me and in real estate sales, that would include lead generating for buyers and sellers, consulting a client toward an investment in real estate, writing and negotiating contracts, and anything that results in creating or preserving income.

If you have trouble determining which activities are red, yellow, or green, consider their dollar value. Red activities generally can be eliminated or delegated to an assistant for a low dollar-per-hour rate. Before assigning dollar values to the other tasks, you need to know how much each activity is worth so you can begin to exchange lower value activity for higher-dollar activity.

After I ask a new struggling salesperson to do the Day Planner Test, they are often startled to discover how nonproductive they are. They haven't yet realized how much time in their day is spent on low-value busyness. They're also astounded to learn how much time they are spending on projects that other people have scheduled for them. Remember, not all powers in the universe are working to help you accomplish your goals. Some people don't mind using your time and energy to accomplish what *they* want.

EITHER YOU PLAN YOUR PERFECT,
PRODUCTIVE AND REWARDING DAY
. . . OR THE OUTSIDE WORLD WILL—IT'S YOUR CHOICE.

In a real estate salesperson's life, as with many sales careers that are commission-based, the highest valued tasks (creating new leads, consulting, closing a sale, etc.) might pay $25, $50 or even $500 per hour depending on the sales price and commission structure. When you identify your hourly target when performing the highest dollar productive tasks versus other things you *could* do, you'll get a better picture of why you're earning the money you earn by using your current day-planning strategy. You'll become very aware about what you *should* do after this analysis. For many tasks, the cost might run between $10 and $20 an hour if they were subcontracted or outsourced. Highly paid salespeople often earn double, triple, or more than ten times that when operating in their twenty percent strength zone exclusively and leaving the details to administrative help.

We have a finite amount of available time and energy. To say "yes" to a highly rewarding and top dollar paying activity, you have to learn to say "no" to things that simply don't support your new strategy. That's sometimes hard if you're a people pleaser, but I've learned that when I respectfully say "no" while explaining my challenge and priorities, people usually understand. I've found this statement to be very helpful: "Thank you for asking. I'd love to help you right now, but I can't give you 100 percent of my attention because I have other commitments. You're important to me. Can we schedule a time later today or tomorrow to connect when I'll be fully present?" The interesting thing is that eighty percent of the time, people solve their own issues, or they don't come back because they realize their issue wasn't really a big deal. Often, some of them just want to chat with me. I've also learned another tactic that works well. I can say, "I'm in the middle of a time-sensitive project, but I really want to help you. Is your challenge a 60-second issue, or will it take longer? If it will take longer, wouldn't it make sense to make an appointment?" People often try to communicate their concern very quickly so I can give them an immediate answer, or they ask for an appointment so we have more time to talk about it. Either way, you stayed the course with *your* priorities for that portion of the day *you* scripted. Similarly, a sign on your office door can explain that you're consumed with a time-sensitive project. Put a sticky note or small dry erase board under the sign so people can leave a name and number for a callback when you come up for air.

Here's the bottom line: if you don't script your life, other people will script it for you. After completing the Day Planner Test, you might find that you need to wriggle out of certain activities that have been planned for you by others.

You begin to take control of your life by taking control of your planner. Remember the challenge from the previous chapter, and repeat after me: "I will not allow the story of my life to be written by other people. I am the author of my own life!"

If you are the author, then write. Don't passively allow other people to take the pen out of your hand and write your life for you. Regaining control happens one hour at a time, one minute at a time, and one commitment at a time. This is the mindset you need as you begin scripting a new life, a life where you are involved in high-dollar, high-worth activities eighty percent of the day.

And while you have your pen out, I want you to try an exercise that will open your mind to new possibilities. I want you to script your perfect workday. During this perfect day, you are hitting all your goals, winning on your scoreboard, working continually in your top twenty percent, and feeling strong and healthy.

What would that day look like? Think it through:

- What time would you wake up?

- What would you spend time doing first? (Do you work out? Spend time with God? Connect with your children? Sing and dance to jump-charge your energy?)

- When you arrive at the office, what high-dollar activities are you engaged in?

- How long do you spend making sales calls?

- Who do you meet with?

- What critical relationships are you building?

- Who do you have lunch with?

- How do you reenergize after lunch?

- What afternoon activities do you engage in?

- Who do you connect with that evening, and what kind of difference are you making in their lives?

Envision your best possible day, and write it all out, being as specific as possible. Then let this "script" be your new guide. Plan your next perfect day by creating a call and contact list before leaving the office. This will allow you to eliminate morning confusion about who to call and what to say. You'll come into the office with a clean desk and a clear plan. Keep the list in front of you, but be forewarned that it may take practice to master scripting and living your perfect day. It's beyond worth it.

Remember, your life and your career are simply a series of days. There is no other way to move forward in your career without moving forward in your daily planning. These executive functions of deciding what is critical and what is nonessential are the difference-makers between average and spectacular.

ENERGY WHEN AND WHERE YOU NEED IT

As you envision your perfect workday, one concept to keep in mind is the idea of maximizing your energy. Ask yourself, *How can I give my best energy to my most important projects? And how can I give the most important people in my life my best and most focused self?*

Dale Carnegie, one of the world's most inspirational and practical self-help gurus, famously said, "Let the winds of enthusiasm sweep through you. Live today with gusto." Couldn't you use a little more gusto in your life?

Gary Keller, founder of Keller Williams, breaks down energy into four categories:

- Spiritual energy,
- Physical energy,
- Emotional energy, and
- Business energy.

I've found that when I determine what fuels me in each of these categories, and then set up my day to provide the right fuel at the right time, I can live my strongest and best day. We all have limited amounts of energy and bandwidth for tackling projects, so I want to use my limited hours, focus, and bandwidth on my most important activities.

Let's look at each category and brainstorm ways to generate the right energy flow for your day.

Spiritual Energy

Starting well in any endeavor is key. It lays the foundation for finishing strong. Starting well, for me, means fueling myself with spiritual energy first because it keeps me from mindlessly throwing energy into the wrong priorities. This includes waking up and focusing my thoughts on what I am grateful for. When I enter a grateful state, I stop the flood of negative thoughts and am reminded that I am here today for something good, something higher than merely reacting to whatever life is hurling at me.

This includes connecting with God and seeing what is truly important. Starting positively with the God of love means I am on a higher plane from the first minutes of the day. God knows what is most important and what is best for me, so when I connect with Him, it prevents small-mindedness on every level. His ways are higher than our ways and His thoughts are higher than our thoughts.[14]

How do you connect with what is most important to you? And just as significantly, *when* do you do this? Do you haphazardly attempt to generate spiritual energy during holidays and vacations? It's not enough, my friend!

I recommend starting every day with strong spiritual energy through prayer, devotionals, meditation, or moments of gratitude. This doesn't require a long or overly religious exercise. Instead, it is a preventative measure, protecting you from the subtlety of negative progression.

Point to your true north each morning. Recalibrate on the highest level first.

Physical Energy

Once I have fueled myself spiritually, I make sure I am fueled physically. This includes attending to nutrition, exercise, and of course, sleep.

Sleep is a major issue for Americans today. Maybe it's because we are bombarded by so many stimuli that our brains never sleep. Maybe we have the misconception that rest is for the weak. But reputable journals regularly warn us about the need for a strong rest routine. In fact, the Centers for Disease Control offers pages of information and advice about the growing crisis of sleep insufficiency. Here is one summary:

> A third of U.S. adults report that they usually get less than the recommended amount of sleep. Not getting enough sleep is linked with many chronic diseases and conditions—such as type 2 diabetes, heart disease, obesity, and depression—that threaten our nation's health. Not getting enough sleep can lead to motor vehicle crashes and mistakes at work, which cause a lot of injury and disability each year. Getting enough sleep is not a luxury—it is something people need for good health. Sleep disorders can also increase a person's risk of health problems. However, these disorders can be diagnosed and treated, bringing relief to those who suffer from them.[15]

But do we really need another announcement from the CDC? We know we need more sleep to live with gusto, to give our best energy to our most important priorities. Some of us have legitimate sleep disorders, but for most of us, getting more sleep is not rocket science. Turn off the TV. Turn off the laptop. Put your phone in "Do Not Disturb" mode. Go to bed in a dark, cool room by 10 P.M. AND SEE WHAT HAPPENS. FOR PEAK PHYSICAL ENERGY, STICK TO A BEDTIME. YOUR BODY AND PRIORITIES WILL THANK YOU THE NEXT DAY.

Of course, physical energy involves much more than sleep. When we skip the gym and start the morning with coffee and donuts, we can't expect to feel peak energy levels throughout the day.

Personally, I need frequent physical activity to create the level of energy I desire. When I have regular physical workouts, it allows me to sweat out the tension, connect better with others, and stay focused longer. My capacity for energy increases with each session with my trainer. I leave our sessions completely juiced and ready to conquer the rest of my day.

But even knowing how the gym fuels me, it's easy to find excuses to skip it, so I work hard to eliminate my excuses. I hate to waste money, so I pay for sessions in advance. This is an incentive for me, but guess what? It's not always enough. I have also arranged for my trainer to text me the night before our sessions. My favorite trainer is Rami Odeh. He's a certified fitness beast who understands psychology too! He sends me encouraging messages like, "Looking forward to a great workout tomorrow at 6:30 A.M.! You won't regret giving yourself this energy boost and you'll love yourself more!" His texts prepare me for a productive workout. They also remind me that someone else is counting on me to be there. Someone will be standing in the gym, alone, waiting for me to show up. If I don't, he'll be disappointed. That's motivation for me. On the other side of the coin, he'll sometimes use a negative reinforcement to inspire me. Something like: "Hey, put down the bag of chips! Are you ready to get serious about your health tomorrow morning at 6:30?" For me, a touch of sarcasm is often more motivating than the positive reinforcement most people prefer. But the truth is that any activity that requires sincere effort also requires motivation . . . and the source of motivation is largely irrelevant.

What motivates you to get moving? Meeting a friend who likes the activities you do for camaraderie and accountability? Checking a box on your spreadsheet? Getting a badge on your workout app? Find the combination of motivators that work for you and keep your physical energy high enough to win your day. Then, when you win day after day, you will see unprecedented progress.

Emotional Energy

The benefits of spiritual and physical energy are well-documented, but emotional energy is a concept we don't often consider. Physically, most of us know what it feels like to carry around a few extra pounds of weight. When I gain too many extra pounds, my feet become sore and my legs ache. I don't move as quickly and easily as I do at my ideal weight. Then, if I don't make any corrections, I adjust to the heavier, more sluggish me. I just become accustomed to dragging those pounds around with me all day.

Emotional weight is similar. It can build up in the form of grudges, resentment, and negative stories we carry around in our minds. And it's exhausting! Whenever we have a negative interaction with someone at home or work, and put off repairing that relationship, we carry that extra weight in the meantime.

We've all heard that resentment is the poison we give ourselves. When we hold on to resentment after conflicts or miscommunications, that negative energy slows us down. It drains energy as we replay those conversation in our minds. And how can you focus on important things when you're stewing over an injustice?

We must clear the air if we ever want to live our best life and put forth our best energy. Otherwise, those unresolved issues will stay with us like extra pounds. It's possible that you've already adjusted to accumulated negative energy to the point that you don't even realize how much bandwidth it's taking up.

Do you want that positive energy back? Then apologize for your part in the conflict. Forgive the other person's injustice. Clear the air. Start over with a clean slate. You'll feel much lighter immediately. When you carry the burden of others' anger or disappointment, you're actually giving up space in your mind that reduces the available space for positive thoughts and energy. There's only so much bandwidth inside you for emotional energy, and you make a choice every moment what to put there. If negative thoughts are omnipresent, it's exhausting. Ironically, much of the time the other person doesn't know or doesn't care that he's had that impact on you. So why allow it? Unless you see it as a choice, you're effectively a prisoner. Let me remind you: you're in control of your thoughts, your words, and your actions . . . and no one else.

I shared with you back in Chapter One about many of the difficulties I faced in childhood with my various parent figures. I'm proud to say that I now have a positive relationship with all those people. I realize they were doing the best they could with the knowledge they had at the time, so I love them now, completely and without any reserve. I also made the conscious effort to confront each of them in loving ways to release the hurt and allow them to acknowledge it. To varying degrees they did, and once released, all that pain literally left my body. The key was that I stayed curious about the reasons for their behavior and maintained my hope to heal the relationship. This is a lesson I began to learn in my twenties when I gained insights from life coaches and therapists.

Group counseling may have been the most therapeutic of all experiences for me. It was amazing how much the experiences of others helped expose and connect the dots with my own challenges. It's a unique way of exploring your inner self vicariously through others in a safe environment. As mentioned before, it's quite possible that your worst day ever could be someone else's best day ever—as crazy as it sounds, I know it's true. Our struggles are very real, and the damage is often horrible, but progress is possible. To some extent, you decide how toxic the experience ultimately becomes and for how long. Grieving, healing, and forgiveness are effective antidotes, including the need to forgive yourself. All of this takes time, but you'll heal much quicker with the help of others who have been down the same road.

I highly recommend quality professional help if the concept of release and forgiveness seems impossible. It was crucial for me, illuminating blind spots and securing a better foundation to build upon. Sometimes knowing what you want to become is a gift, but it's even more powerful to identify what you *don't* want to become.

Ultimately, I've learned that if I had chosen to hold grudges against those who hurt me, it would have done far more harm to me than to them. If you can't forgive an offense out of the goodness of your heart, you should do it anyway, for your own benefit. Only after you forgive others will you be able to free yourself of any negative emotional energy you're carrying around.

In addition to mending relationships, emotional energy can be increased through proactively seeking positive and uplifting conversations with others. See for yourself. Give three people honest and heartfelt compliments today, and then notice your energy level. You will get an immediate energy boost! It is impossible to stay down when you lift others up. As you encourage other people, energy flows to both of you.

I recently heard Chad Hymas speak at a leadership conference. At the age of twenty-seven he was crushed by a 2000-pound bale of hay. Miraculously, he lived, but was left paralyzed. "When things like this happen," he told us, "You start showing people you love them."

To demonstrate, he asked to borrow a cellphone from a guy in the audience and then asked if he could send a text to the man's wife. We all sat in stunned silence as Chad sent this message: "I am grateful that you are my wife. I am so glad that we have such amazing children. They are a credit to you and your character. Thank you for covering for me today so I can attend this conference. Can't wait to share today. Miss you. Love you."

Her response was, "Who stole your phone?"

Would your loved ones respond the same way? Would expressing love and encouragement seem out of character for you? Try giving the gift of honest appreciation and gratitude to those around you, and watch your own life improve in the process.

This morning after my devotional time, I was going through some mail and saw a letter from my son's college. It was his report card, and his lowest grade was a 94. I wasn't surprised. He truly applies himself at school, studying three or four hours per day. I almost set the report card aside, but instead decided to take a picture of it and text him. I wrote, "I am so proud of you. You have always been the kind of kid who works hard and achieves your goals. There is no telling what the future holds for you. You are awesome!"

I think I got more out of giving the compliment than he got from receiving it. I felt awesome just typing it! Give the gift of kind words and you will receive a present as well, a present of emotional energy to fuel your day. Being loving and generous with kind words towards others is a "superpower" to you and a gift to them.

Business Energy

Spiritual energy keeps you pointed to your true north. Physical energy abounds when you are physically active and getting enough rest and sleep. Emotional energy results when you are in the right state of mind because you have good interpersonal relationships with the people in your circle of influence. Once those things are done, you are ready to engage in positive business energy.

How do you manage your business energy throughout the workday? There is only one way: Give your best energy to your most important work. And your best energy is your first energy. It's also important to stage a productive workspace environment. Put only the necessities in front of you to avoid distractions, and stage them in a way that inspires your peak attention and performance. Standing desks are awesome. They keep you moving so they promote better health. Position all the tools of your work within reach, and utilize technology to enable you to enjoy maximum efficiency as you move through your key tasks.

It's also important to minimize distractions by isolating yourself from the things and people that might pull you off task. For instance, if you're required to call new clients (a.k.a., generate leads), make sure you have a client relationship management system with notes that are easy to find, use and track. Also make sure that *before* you go home each day, you create your contact list (with numbers attached so you don't have to look for them later) for the following day so you can go straight the most vital calls as soon as you arrive in the office. This strategy helps you avoid the distraction of figuring out who to call when you get to the office, only to be interrupted by another person with a plea to solve their problem as you wander aimlessly back to the kitchen for another cup of coffee, hoping to regroup before too long. Make a habit of time blocking—put planning and technology to work for you and focus on the 20% that matters most every day . . . and watch your success level climb!

If lead generation is the most critical work for your business, tackle it first. Schedule three to four hours at the beginning of your workday to generate leads. Don't be sidetracked by email, newsletters, or office organizing first, leaving only second-hand energy for the daunting task of making calls. Treat each day like the day before you go on vacation. I don't know about you, but the day before I leave for a week or two away from the office seems to bring out my best. It's as if I installed a turbo charger into my focus! Imagine having that energy every day! I once had a top agent share that his best weeks are always the ones leading up to a vacation. Not only did sales pour in, but his attention to the "big rocks" became an elevated priority, leaving nothing undone as he headed for the airport. I jokingly suggested he schedule more vacations!

What if you attack each day is if you had your boss or most successful client looking over your shoulder all day, shadowing you to discover your secrets to success. You'd be unstoppable! Even if you had that mentality a couple of days a week, you'd be far more successful. This concept works equally well when you hire high-performing talent for your team. You always want them to see you in your best light. That's why winning teams tend to keep winning. Stellar performance is expected from each person. Teamwork and accountability keep everyone on the right track.

Pro Tip: *Do your important work in the morning. And do the hard jobs first.*

Once you've thought through the need for spiritual, physical, emotional, and business energy, you might want to go back and tweak the script for your perfect day just a bit. Time blocking is the key to effectively managing business energy. As you attempt to structure a perfect workday, you'll need to ensure that you're creating relationships

MAKE THE MOST OF EVERY DAY | 179

that matter before you get caught up in menial tasks that offer very little reward. We've already taken a quick look at Brian Tracy's book, *Eat that Frog*. He makes several insightful comments about this issue, including:

> You can get your time and your life under control only to the degree to which you discontinue lower-value activities.
> And,
> The critical determinant of the quality of your relationships is the amount of time that you spend face-to-face with the people you love, and who love you in return.[16]

Your goal is to make progress in all four categories. Create a progressive experience, and your goals are within reach. If you are clear about what fuels you in each category, you are going to do the work. Wake up every day and take the first step. Fuel each category, and then each category will fuel you.

In his book, *The Miracle Morning*, Hal Elrod uses the acronym SAVERS to shape a productive day. The letters stand for Scribe (write your hopes, goals, and plans for the day), Affirmations (give yourself a pep talk), Visualizations (imagine what progress will look like at the end of the day), Exercise (get those muscles moving), Read (soak up encouragement and insights), and Silence (practice solitude and quiet to create a sense of calm). After Hal barely survived a horrific car accident, the gift of more years of life prompted him to reevaluate his priorities and savor every moment. He writes, *"You are always exactly where you are supposed to be, experiencing what you need to experience, to learn what you must learn, in order to become the person you need to be to create the life you truly want. Always."*[17]

There are only two reasons people change: inspiration or desperation. It's wise to choose inspiration, but desperation certainly gets our attention!

A DAILY WAR

The battle to achieve your goals is fought daily. And although we often build huge goal lists for each year, it's won daily as well. Scripting your perfect workday gives you a battle plan. Fueling up with spiritual, physical, emotional, and business energy provides the strength and stamina to withstand everyday pressures, problems, and setbacks. And scorekeeping every day ensures that you're staying on track and not beginning to falter in your efforts. When you win enough days, you'll win weeks, which lead to game-winning and goal-fulfilling months. String those together and you'll crush your annual goals, one hyper-productive day at a time.

Lifestyle authority Aubrey Marcus challenges his readers to learn how to get the most from their bodies and minds each day. He writes, "To live one day well is the same as to live ten thousand days well. To master twenty-four hours is to master your life."[18]

When you string together enough winning days in a row, you will win big time! Win the day, friend, and do it *every* day!

QUESTIONS TO CONSIDER:

1. Are you spending too much time doing low-level activities that could be outsourced or sub-contracted? How do you know?

2. What did you learn from your Day Planner Test? Where are you currently investing most of your time, and how can you create more time to devote to urgent and important matters?

After you script your perfect workday, what's the first thing you need to do to initiate significant daily improvements?

Do you have extreme accountability each day to stay on point and focus on the "big rocks"? And is your environment conducive to success (consider people, technology and logistics)?

4. How do you typically begin each morning? Does it set the tone for a productive and rewarding day?

5. What changes do you need to make to ensure you maintain a high level of spiritual, physical, and emotional energy throughout the day?

CHAPTER 9

MAKING BETTER CONNECTIONS

Leadership expert Jim Rohn famously observed, "You are the average of the five people you spend the most time with," and I couldn't agree more. Most people are influenced by the attitudes, habits, and success levels of the people in their inner circle much more than they realize. Put another way, the quality of your life usually correlates directly to the quality of the people in it. These are the ones you trust to give you the input and feedback you need to stay on the road to success in every aspect of your life. They also add or reduce the amount of positive energy and inspiration in your personal environment.

You'd think that these days it would be easier than ever to connect with other people, thanks to ever-improving technology, websites that attract devotees of seemingly any personal interest (music, hobbies, vocation, travel, etc.), the ability to Zoom or FaceTime into another person's home, and more. Yet somehow the distance between people seems to be growing rather than decreasing.

Let's use texting as an example. It's an efficient method of transferring information, to be sure, yet it isn't a relationship-building way to communicate. It doesn't serve to bond people due to its one-dimensional format. To begin with, written text eliminates other crucial aspects of communication. When texting, we never have the benefit of seeing facial expressions, body language, and other nonverbal clues of what the sender wants to communicate. Not to mention, texting offers only what we can *see*. We have five senses, and sight is only one of them. Don't you ever miss hearing the other person's laughter, or smelling her perfume? How much do we miss all those times we could choose to communicate in person, but opt for the convenience of texting instead?

And have you ever had a conflict with someone via text? It's pointless and dangerous. In addition to the lost visual clues and the complete disregard for proper capitalization and punctuation, you have no *verbal* cues at all. When you can't hear someone's tone of voice or how they enunciate their words, how can you be sure of their intention? I'm sure we've all misinterpreted someone's texts more than once.

I suspect technology is depriving our younger generation of the art of working through disagreements and still staying friends. I learned those lessons in the back of a 1970s station wagon as my brothers and I fought the entire way to and from Florida on family vacations! Disagreements would start out innocently enough, but in the pre-Google era, we were often unable to settle the matter on the spot. We would argue about sports statistics, geographic facts, world events, and just about anything we could think of. But without an authority to prove one person right and the other person wrong, our intensity would increase until we could get to an Encyclopedia Britannica or one of the adults in the front seat made an authoritative ruling. The loser of that argument would get another lesson in humility and how to deal with rejection. But in the meantime, we both honed the skills of verbal banter, salesmanship, and persuasion.

Today's arguments between teens go like this:

"Hey, did you know our spaceships just found footprints on Mars?"

"No they didn't. That's stupid."

Then both parties pull out their phones, and one of them is proved right within seconds. Settling trivia questions quickly is okay, I suppose, yet I fear that a lot of firm beliefs are shot down in seconds, when more benefit would come from longer, ongoing discussion and debate.

I realize technology isn't going away, and I'm seeing artificial intelligence (AI) used more frequently as a huge marketing tool. Regardless, I believe the highest level of relationship is still face to face, belly to belly, and toe to toe! If I want to deescalate an argument with a peer, client, or family member, I find the time to address it head-on and in person. The energy is always better if the other person sees that my energy is nonjudgmental. I just want to work out the problem and come to a mutually agreeable solution.

UPGRADING YOUR NETWORK

The influence of the people you surround yourself with may be so subconscious that you aren't even aware of how each person is changing you . . . or worse, *not* changing you. But it can be hard to connect with new people.

The world has made most of us naturally suspicious of others, and rightfully so! I'm not even talking about the "stranger danger" of aggressive panhandlers or shady-looking figures lurking on a dimly lit street after dark. It's getting harder and harder for me to trust everyday salespeople. Who hasn't been deceived by false promotions or high-pressure tactics into buying something they ultimately didn't want or need? What I've learned is that *all* people want to buy, but no one wants to be sold a shoddy bill of goods. How often do you walk into a retail store to be met with the universal question, "May I help you?" to which you reply, "Just looking, thank you!" The truth may be that you *do* want help—just not the kind that corners you into buying something you don't need. Consumers all want to buy; they just don't want to be sold! (Note to salespeople and customer service professionals: that simply means talking less, listening more, and asking great questions. You'll be far more successful if you add value, build trust, and align what you're promoting with what they need. It's an unselfish contribution, and we all appreciate that.)

Even business and casual relationships require a reasonable degree of trust. And when you're deciding which people you want influence you, that need for trust skyrockets. You want people who can offer a lot of expertise, but trust is even more essential. Those you are closest to have to feel safe sharing with you, trusting you'll keep confidences and help them unselfishly. With that in mind, let's start giving some thought to the people you'd like to include in your inner circle. After you create your inner circle, your inner circle creates you.

Have you ever overheard your spouse chat with a friend or family member on the phone? As the conversation progresses, you may hear slight changes in his or her way of speaking. If the person at the other end is in a different part of the country, your spouse's accent may change to match that person's. If the other person tends to speak loudly, your spouse may increase volume as well. You don't even notice it when you're the one on the phone, but those around you can't miss it.

This is just another subtle example of how those we spend the most time with have influence on us that we don't even realize. Consequently, we need to be wise and discerning when choosing those people.

Make a list of family members, friends, coworkers, and neighbors who currently fill your inner circle. Then focus on one name at a time and ask yourself, *Do I want to become more like this person? If I spend the next ten years hanging out with this person, what will my life look like?*

These people comprise your current *network*. How many of them are dysfunctional? How many are physically out of shape? Do they all inspire and encourage you, or are some of them incurable pessimists? I'm not suggesting you ditch your friends because they eat carbs, watch excessive pointless TV, or are occasionally in a bad mood, but given the likelihood that you'll become more and more like those you network with, you need to be honest. Further analyze the names on your list using these questions to form three categories:

- Does this person elevate my thinking and behavior?
- Is he or she simply neutral, neither helping nor hurting me?
- Is this person hindering my thinking and my goals?

My friend Shaun Rawls, the author of the book, *"F"-It-Less*, shared a grid that was helpful when I analyzed team members.[19] The key is to determine what you will and won't accept, and then stand firm on these values regardless of a person's talent or any other extraneous reasons. For me, Positive Energy is a non-negotiable and High Potential a close second! Energy is infectious; it applies to negative and positive sources of energy. We're all mirrors who reflect the light others shine on us, so be very careful to notice the frequency and sources of energy, personally and professionally. In this exercise, talent and the capacity to perform in a role vital to organizational success are described as "potential." Here's a grid with the categories for you to analyze your inner circle. Where do your key people land on it?

Low Potential/Negative Energy	High Potential/Negative Energy
Low Potential/Positive Energy	High Potential/Positive Energy

After placing people where you think they fit best, what did you learn about your team? My guess is that you don't have many in the high energy/high potential box. You can never have too many in that box, but you can certainly have too many in the other boxes. The point of this exercise is to be honest about who's in your inner circle so you can think more clearly about your standards. Some made your path to success more rewarding, but some are roadblocks or detours. This exercise can be a turning point for you as a leader.

If anyone in one of the other three boxes has the potential to move into the High Potential/High Energy quadrant, create a plan to equip and place that person for a better future.

You are in charge of what you will or won't allow in your world (professionally and personally), so make sure it's by design and to your standard. Don't be afraid to challenge people by setting high standards, but be sure to have regular, authentic conversations so the standards you've created are understood and honored by everyone. In those conversations, share your observations about the team member, ask questions and listen carefully. Also, be a good role model by asking for honest feedback about your own behavior and the team. I love the book *Fierce Conversations* by Susan Scott. She lays out a plan for open and honest conversations like the ones I'm suggesting. My favorite two quotes are: "Let the silence do the heavy lifting" after asking a really good question, and the other is "No one denies their own truth." When you ask great questions and allow people to answer for themselves, they will never deny that truth. Honesty and transparency increase the level of trust, which usually leads to higher performance. Great leaders are great listeners.

PEOPLE ARE RESISTANT WHEN THEY DON'T FEEL HEARD AND UNDERSTOOD, BUT WHEN THEY KNOW THEY'RE UNDERSTOOD, THEY OFTEN ARE OPEN TO STEPS OF IMPROVEMENT.

Surround yourself with people you respect and like—not just those who agree with you all the time. When you dominate people, you deprive the relationships of reciprocal growth, and someone usually has to micromanage them. When that happens, they bring minimal value to the team beyond their core job requirements. You want people with high-level skills, work and life experience, a strong work ethic, uncommon commitment and an amazing motivation to support the team!

Beyond the hard skills required for each role, you need people who are natural connectors with the ability to empathize. It's really easy to work with people who have a high degree of EQ as well as IQ. The term EQ, emotional quotient, relates to one's ability to understand, use and manage your own emotions in positive ways to relieve stress, communicated effectively, empathize with others and defuse conflict. IQ is raw intelligence and is a wonderful asset since "you can't teach smart," but the real find is a person with a blend of intelligence and emotional awareness, coupled with a a passion for the organization and their role in it. That's the grand slam team member!

You won't have to worry about controlling people if your team members are talented and bring positivity to every conversation while staying honest and authentic. They'll know how to manage healthy disagreement for the betterment of the team and will leave others feeling heard and appreciated.

Here's the bottom line: If you notice you have a lot of people in your inner circle who are hindering your progress, it is critical to dilute their influence by adding more high-quality thinkers that are learning-based and generally growth-minded. The people you choose for your network have tremendous value in your life. If your current network isn't helping you get where you want to go, you must create a new one.

You've already asked yourself, *Where do I want to go?* At this point the question becomes, "Who is already there? Who is doing what I want to do, and doing it extraordinarily well?" If your inner circle isn't packed with people who are doing something better than you, then you're not moving upward. You're either stagnant or moving backward.

Awesome people know awesome people. You are awesome, so find other highly skilled and productive people who can move you to a new level in every area, who also bring positive energy. Go back to your Life Wheel. Move from category to category, and for each one, write the names of people you know whom you would like to spend more time with.

I recently attended a conference called GoBundance, a mastermind group of wealthy thinkers. While there, I met a physical trainer who encouraged me to test my body to determine the ratio of water to muscle to fat. He and I spent an hour discussing the breakdown of my personal health.

In only one hour with such an expert, I had a breakthrough! I'd had a goal to lose forty pounds, but he informed me that my muscle ratio was extremely high. Instead, he recommended that I focus on losing only about twenty pounds of fat, and he gave me some truly helpful suggestions that I am implementing now.

Before meeting this trainer, I couldn't have come up with the right plan to improve my health. No one else in my current network could move me forward. I needed a new addition to my network, and this trainer was perfect! As a result, I'm now reducing my consumption of red wine and alcohol (which is really hard for me because I love wine!), changing my workout routine, and making some logical adjustments in my diet. Small yet intentional steps will take you to your highest goals if you stay focused and committed.

If your Life Wheel reveals areas where you aren't satisfied, then your network is clearly incomplete. The secret to success is found in connecting with knowledgeable people—not googling for the quickest answer. I succeed with people and through people. These connections have made all the difference in my life, and it is only one result of asking "Who?" instead of "How?"

In Chapter Six I told you about meeting Dave Pridemore, the founder of Camp Grace, and our mutual desire to serve underprivileged kids. What I didn't say is that at the time, I needed a spiritual guide, and I believe God brought Dave and me together. Dave ministered to me tirelessly during a very low point in my life. Since then, he has helped me improve my life in many ways as he elevates my thinking and my prayer life. I make a point to stay connected to him, to meet with him regularly, and to continue learning from him.

If you examine the list of people in your network and don't believe they can take you where you want to go, then it's time to revise your network. But where do you start?

TWENTY-FOUR AREAS FOR BUILDING AND EXPANDING YOUR INFLUENCE

Over the years, I've created a list of great places to grow your network that I provide to my team and now share with you. Make plans to go to as many of these places as possible to meet, connect with, and expand your inner circle.

1. *Chamber of Commerce or Local Business Owners' Meetings.* Who's doing business in your community? These are places to connect with the movers and shakers of your community.

2. *Rotary Club, Lions Club, Optimist Club, Moose Club, etc.* Clubs are terrific sources of potential associates if you find one aligned with your purpose.

3. *Social Media*. Who's your target audience? Where do they go to hang out online? Facebook, Twitter, LinkedIn, Instagram, Pinterest, blogs, and other popular sites can help you find people with interests very similar to yours.

4. *Toastmasters*. This is a place to meet motivated people *and* get better at public speaking. Maximize your capacity to inspire and lead meetings from these skilled communicators.

5. *Specialty Groups*. Find and quickly connect with people who have common cultural interests, whether women, men, Asian, Hispanic, gay, country of origin, etc.

6. *Nonprofits*. Make a difference while you connect in an existing group. Then, if so inclined, take it to the next level by starting your own nonprofit or chairing a board. Social credibility rises if you add value to the mission of those fighting for the good of the community or world.

7. *Community Organizations*. Serve in a leadership role on a homeowner's association or some other local special-interest group.

8. *Alumni Groups*. You'll find fierce loyalty among the alums of high schools, colleges, and other institutions of learning.

9. *Private Clubs* (social and business). Look for opportunities in country clubs, investor clubs, and other such groups. Do more than just join. Be sure to connect, engage, and add value to the group. In time, the seeds you sow will grow into quality relationships that help you reach your goals.

10. *Religious Institutions*. Churches, synagogues, mosques, temples, etc. usually attract people eager to help others. (Seeking

connections shouldn't be the primary purpose for going to religious services, but for those who regularly attend, it can be a side benefit.)

11. *Meetup.com.* Use on-line tools like this one to help you meet people for social or business networking. Groups are available in all major cities. I've even heard of people using dating sites to find friends.

12. *Business Networking Groups.* Check out sites like BNI.com (Business Network International) or Powercore.net. Both are powerful business-specific referral groups. They were created for building businesses and sharing referrals, but I've made many life-long friends over the years in these meetings.

13. *Industry-Specific Events.* I like to attend events sponsored by my company and outside affiliates as well from my industry. I particularly like attending events outside of my market area for greater diversity and less concern for local market competition. I want to network and meet the people who have risen to the top there. This is a great way to expand your circle of influence and add to your sources for potential mentors.

14. *Educational and Motivational Seminars and Events.* Get to know thought leaders and up-and-comers in in the area of motivation and tactical skills for success. Go to trade shows, attend seminars and meet all the people you can. You never know which one will give you just the bit of information you need to accomplish a long-standing goal. Motivated and generous people often show up at workshops and seminars. As an example, I'm a member of GoBundance, an organization committed to sharing best practices in living a full life and winning with real estate investments. (www.gobundance.com)

15. *Travel Groups.* Get diverse perspectives from international groups and country-of-origin networks.

16. *Hobby Groups.* Looking for an authority on some specific topic? Look to hobbyists for sound advice for gardening, knitting, model planes, music, art, cooking . . . you name it.

17. *Sports Groups.* Most sports have dedicated groups of fans at different levels of interest—recreational, college, or pro.

18. *Client Parties and Special Events.* Your clients have seen who you are and how you perform. They might be able to connect you with others who have impressed them. Create events for them to reconnect with you and other clients, add value and watch the magic happen!

19. *Festivals and Special Events.* If it supports your business, sponsor a booth to promote your purpose, services, distinct capabilities, and brand.

20. *Schools.* Support your local PTA, school sports and academic teams, and other school functions.

21. *Personal Contacts.* It sounds obvious, but not everyone thinks to ask their regular (though perhaps only occasional) contacts for help with life goals. Consider corporate connections from previous jobs as well as your doctors, lawyers, accountants, and other industry professionals you know.

22. *Vendors and Alliance Partners.* What are other professions that align with yours and serve the same pool of customers that you do?

23. *Classes.* Arrange to teach classes in neighboring market areas or cities. Connect with other leaders to share expertise, insight,

MAKING BETTER CONNECTIONS | 195

and experience for the betterment of others. Share your gifts and you'll love yourself more . . . and so will your friends and colleagues.

Pro Tip: *To really master a topic, commit to teaching it after you've developed expertise!*

24. *Local Informal Gathering Places.* Consider restaurants, bars, juice bars, coffee shops, and similar settings where people meet. Offer to promote the establishment to your social and work sphere. I've found that many are open to creating a coupon for a two-for-one dinner, free appetizer, or dessert for a first-time visitor. The eating establishment gets new business, and I connect with more of my customers and clients!

Pick and choose from these twenty-four options, start making new connections, and watch your network grow! Being proactive and intentional beats organic and lucky ten out of ten times. There's also quality in the quantity. Weed through the people you don't want to affiliate with, but pay attention to those you do . . . and watch the magic happen.

SOMETHING TO OFFER

You've asked yourself "Where am I going?" and "Who's already there who might be able to help me?" If your goal is to be known by those whom you would like to add to your network, then your third question is, "How can I contribute to the lives of these influencers? What can I add of value?"

When you come from a position of contribution where your only goal is to help those around you with no strings attached, you can't lose. The challenge is to figure out how to create opportunities to benefit those you have identified. Sometimes it's as easy as asking, "How is your day going? How can I make it better?"

Contributing to the lives of those influencers doesn't need to be complicated. Simple contribution includes holding the door for a person, sending a thank-you note, or giving a compliment. All forms of contribution tip the scales in your favor. All forms of thoughtfulness and gratitude count!

Pleasant experiences are gifts you can give the people in your life throughout the year. A good experience is what is called a "touch." I call this habit "making deposits" because you don't cash any checks until you've made enough deposits to cover them.

At Keller Williams Realty we use a formula and algorithm for all aspects of business in pursuit of success. When it comes to connecting with people in service-oriented business (consumer-based sales), the size of the database of people you need to know is determined by the number of sales you need to achieve your goals, and it's tied to the quality of those consistent contacts or communications. This concept applies to industries and businesses that rely on a growing client base of raving fans. If repeat and referral-based growth is important to your business, this concept is invaluable.

Based on average conversion percentages, if you want to sell twenty homes in a year, you'd need 120 contacts who know, like and trust you. You can also enhance conversion by adding greater relevant value and building a reputation of success that leads to repeat business and referrals. One key consideration is frequency and quality of the touch or connection. According to KW's research, that number should be thirty-three to thirty-six times per year. To accomplish that, I need to spend approximately three hours per day reaching out and trying to inspire others. I want to connect with people thirty-six times each year, personally through phone calls and events, as well as by using automated emails, texts, newsletters, and other broadcast communications. But nothing rivals the impact of face-to-face connections.

Networking is both art and science. Like a painter, we learn how to use just the right color and tone in our communication to make the best impression, but we also can follow sound and simple metrics, for instance, "Good people know good people." I love the script, "You are amazing, and amazing people know amazing people. Who do you know that I should know, someone who might appreciate the friendship and support we have for each other?" Proactive lead generation for business and personal friendships should be synonymous.

The root of the word "inspire" is related to *aspire*, "to breathe life into." How do you know when someone needs encouragement? According to Zig Ziglar, it's "if they are breathing." Kindness is the currency of humanity. Investing in others by building them up is a gift, and the law of reciprocity will bring kindness back to you!

How many hours do you spend each day trying to improve the lives of those around you? How much time do you spend contributing? How intentional are you at connecting, communicating value, and ferreting out new opportunities to serve? How many can you inspire and uplift in a month or a year?

Marshall Chiles is a comedian and author in Atlanta. He is not only funny, but also quite business savvy having built one of the south's most successful comedy venues. He also owns a company that helps marketers and salespeople infuse more humor into their media and presentations. His book. *Your Presentation is a Joke*, provides a refreshing angle about engaging people in business. I love to be around this guy! He brings joy, wit, and humor into my life, and I most certainly appreciate it. Best of all, he's a thinker who constantly ponders how to make the world a better place. He has invested many hours at homeless shelters for women with children, and it impresses me when people like him lean in for chances to serve. We both engage in helping others as often as possible. We love to talk business and brainstorm ways to go beyond *handouts* to offer a *hand up* to support those in need. I want (and need) more challenging and generous people like Marshall in my life. They teach me to give more than I take.

Contributing to the lives of those around you requires thoughtfulness and intentionality, but it's worth every minute! Ask yourself the following questions to get to a place of contribution:

- "How do I make this person feel whole, heard, and honored?"
- "How do I create a win-win?"
- "How can I give this person the gift of a better experience?"

The good news is that the world is round; every good feeling, donation, or small kindness will come back to you.

TIPS TO CONSIDER WHEN NETWORKING IN A GROUP SETTING

Companies frequently invest in getting to know people personally, regardless of the financial and business outcome. They often use larger events, but they may also connect individually. To help you succeed in your networking efforts, I have compiled a list of my favorite tips for making sure that you are reaching out, helping others, and continuously coming from a place of connection. These tips are mostly business-oriented, but they work in all situations.

5. *Be first in and last out* (FILO). Get to know as many people as possible at every event. It would be a shame to miss the most impactful person of the evening who arrived late . . .

right after you left early! Typically, you'll find smaller crowds early and late, making it easier to have one-on-one conversations. If you know who's coming in advance, do your social media homework to learn all you can about them professionally and personally. Come prepared with insightful questions and connect with them early.

6. *You only get one first impression.* Make it good, lasting, and positive. Credibility is vital. The key to effective connecting is to smile, extend a firm and confident handshake (not a death squeeze), and make frequent eye contact.

7. *Master your listening skills.* Remember the acronym WAIT: "Why Am I Talking?" Don't try so hard to be interesting. Be interested instead.

8. *Dress for success every day.* You should be careful not to underestimate anyone based on the way *they're* dressed, but that doesn't mean they won't reach the wrong conclusion about you if your attire doesn't meet their standards. Besides, you never know when you might meet a multimillion-dollar client or someone with the power to help you land a new job opportunity or promotion.

9. *Make sure your business card and any collateral you share projects the image you desire.* Long after your personal connection, your business card will speak for you. Heavy card stock with rich color and a solid feel not only makes a good first impression, but also serves as a testament to your service and professionalism. In real estate, a photo on the card proves to be valuable. I receive countless cards and toss most of them, but I keep the ones that make me remember the person who gave it to me.

10. *Remain standing.* Standing up reminds you to work the room. It also facilitates a graceful exit if one guest is droning on in endless meaningless conversation. It's also wise to have a script for moving on without offending someone. I say something like, "Hey, this has been great, but I don't want to take up all your time. Thank you so much for taking time to talk to me."

11. *Stand out in a crowd . . . in a positive way.* If you're in a group like Business Networking International, Rotary or some other reoccurring business-minded setting, the discussions can be a bit monotonous at times. When you have an opportunity to speak, change it up! If you express yourself with both creativity and relevance, you're sure to be memorable.

12. *Avoid raunchy topics and jokes that are in poor taste.* Be particularly careful what you post on social media. In trying to be funny to impress your friends, you may end up offending a client or potential employer. Such carelessness can cost you dearly.

13. *Whenever possible, find common interests.* Connecting with people in your network is much easier if you find things you have in common. Not only do your common bonds make a great conversation starter, but you have natural reminders to follow up whenever future situations or current events involve your mutual interests.

14. *Make others feel special, heard, and appreciated.* The quickest and best way to do this is to remember their names. "I'm not good with names" is no excuse. Get better at it. I find that asking for a business card to visually see the name helps, and I try to repeat it two or three times during the conversation.

When possible, I connect the name with a feature or word association that helps me recall it. I often save it in my phone along with a word or business association as a reminder. If it links to a photo in social media, even better!

15. *If you are allowed to present, punctuate your presentation with success stories.* People may not remember all the facts and figures you give them, but they'll recall how you saved the day for a client or helped a former customer when no one else could. People care about what you do, but they care even more when you explain *why* you do it, when it's delivered with humility. (Simon Sinek expands on that concept in his books and Ted Talks.) As the old adage goes, "People may forget what you say, but they never forget how you made them feel." Great stories capture attention and leave an impression. I share stories of my successes, but also of my failures (which are much more interesting to most people), and I relate the lessons I learned from those experiences that benefitted me, my team, and our clients.

16. *Do your research.* Before meeting with anyone new, see what you can find out about the person through Facebook, LinkedIn, Google, etc. for articles or news. Look for any common interests and/or topics to avoid.

17. *Always be ready to present your elevator speech.* Time restraints will sometimes prevent you from giving a full presentation with all its bells and whistles. When asked to *quickly* present a brief overview to a group or individual, be ready to go with a sixty-second summary, one that can be delivered during an elevator ride. It should cover all the basics: your name, your company, what separates you from the competition, and what you're

proposing. The secret is to create a touch of intrigue. When people ask me what I do for a living, I no longer call myself a realtor (there are thousands of them fighting for business); instead, I tell people I'm a "wealth builder" because then they often ask me to explain what that means. I tell them that I specialize in real estate investment, and that I'm convinced all truly wealthy people have real estate in their portfolios. Then I ask, "How's *your* portfolio coming along?" Whatever your business, you can create an intriguing opening statement that causes people to ask for more information. The bottom line is that your first impression will be a big first step in a new relationship, regardless of your product or service.

18. *Have a follow-up plan for everyone you meet.* Automate as much as you can to ensure you do this! Texts and email are fine in most situations to express gratitude, but a personal call is even better, and nothing outweighs the power of a personal handwritten note.

19. *Keep an eye out for special news articles or tools that are relevant to your clients.* It costs nothing and takes very little effort to clip an article and forward it to someone who will appreciate it, yet shows you remember and care about what interests them.

20. *Reward favors.* When people give me leads or referrals, I try to reward them quickly with a small gift or privilege. They've done their part; what comes of it is up to me. Reward the positive behavior and the outcome. Obviously, if the referral leads to a profitable outcome, I follow up with a more significant reward.

21. *Send personal notes.* As mentioned earlier and worth repeating, few expressions have the impact of a heartfelt and sincere

personal note. I have a file where I keep special personal notes I've received. Send five personal notes a day and watch your relationships grow deeper and richer!

22. *Return all calls—every day.* Responsiveness shows respect for your callers. And even if it seems redundant, always send follow-up notes after a new contact is made to cement your professionalism and caring spirit.

23. *Honor commitments, be on time, and come ready to add value.* By "on time" I mean "early." As important as I believe this guideline is, I've had problems with punctuality. In my determination to outwork and outperform others, I used to pack too many commitments into a single day and wouldn't always be on time. As I've matured, I've realized that arriving at appointments early is a gift to myself, relieving much personal anxiety created by the stress of traffic and what tardiness was doing to my reputation. A good friend recently reminded me that arriving early doesn't equate to wasted time. I now get a lot of work done while in waiting areas or in my car out front, waiting for the meeting to start. Adopt the mindset that being early is on time.

24. *Treat all people professionally, but not equally.* Remember the 80/20 rule. Always maintain a respectful and gracious approach to everyone, but devote most of your attention to the twenty percent of your customers and clients who typically create eighty percent of the net results.

25. *Find a mentor . . . and become one.* Don't resist asking someone to mentor you into becoming a better person. But then do the same for someone else younger or in need of support. Being

mentored and mentoring someone else will both contribute to your personal growth and expand your trusted network.

26. *Host first-class events.* Be the one who creates experiences and opportunities, and your influence will rise significantly. The event may be purely social, or it could have an important strategic purpose. Become known as the person people count on to host an event and support your community.

27. *Focus on benefits.* When asking promoting the opportunity to work with you and your company, emphasize how clients benefit rather than you and your services. If I want to sell a home with a fireplace, the fireplace is just a feature. I prefer to sell the benefit: how romantic it would be on a chilly evening to dim the lights, put Barry White on the stereo, and have a crackling fire at their feet. Similarly, in seeking referrals, I don't bluntly inquire about other houses to sell. Instead, I ask, "Do you know anyone interested in building wealth through real estate—either buying, selling, or investing?" Wealth building is a benefit that tends to get people's attention. Clients might not ask out loud, but they are usually wanting to know, "What's in it for me?" Are you promoting features? Or benefits?

28. *Be observant, creative and specific when possible.* In my business, I'm aware that everyone is looking for referrals, so I try to find different ways to ask. For example, I might say if communicating in a group setting where promoting yourself is appropriate, "I've noticed you all have amazing teeth. I'm on a mission to help dentists and their clients build wealth in real estate. Do you know anyone who might be interested, or who has a need I can solve?"

29. *Specialize.* It's a competitive world, and you want to stand out in a crowd. What do you do better than most others in your profession? Lead with that. You want the person to remember, "He's the guy [or "She's the lady"] who's the best at . . ." Specialists are more memorable . . . and they usually earn more than generalists.

30. *Prepare a testimonial letter template ahead of time.* Use the letter to share your network with others as an introduction. When someone responds well to you, ask him or her to send a copy to their database. Even better, get their database and send it for them!

31. *Be strategic in building your network.* Keep a sharp eye out on people who have a positive influence and get things done. Don't ask them for help. Instead, ask how you can help them. Get to know them, find out what their dreams are, and connect them to people and organizations that will be valuable resources. Reconnect regularly with those who are on your top line of contacts.

32. *Have a list of questions to ask a person of influence to ensure the moment isn't wasted.* Don't leave it to chance. Honor them with a statement like, "This is an honor, and I really wanted to be prepared. Would you be offended if I ask a few important questions I scripted in advance?"

Before you end your day, work on your touch and communication strategy for the following day. Have a stack of thank-you cards ready to sign and a list of people you plan to call. Don't wait until the next morning because chaos inevitably ensues, and those plans will be forgotten in the rush.

I realize all these tips are a lot to absorb in one sitting, but I hope you found several you're eager to try out right away. You can always come back and review them from time to time to ensure you're doing all you can to keep strengthening your network.

What's the ideal path to maximize your networking efforts? First, make sure the setting is conducive and appropriate for making contacts. Then remember that the goal is *connecting*—not selling (even if you hope at some point to benefit from your connections). Manipulation is a unilateral strategy, and most businesspeople will see right through it. But if you're sincere about wanting to add value and help every single person to the best of your abilities, you'll win in the end. The law of reciprocity is real: givers get. The key is to start with giving and be patient as you wait for what you're hoping to receive; it'll come if you're authentic and don't demand it or push for it. Try it, you'll see!

Be strategic in building your network of influencers one-on-one. Make it a point to have two or three meetings a week (lunch and breakfast meetings are easiest and less expensive than dinners) with people of influence in your community. Remember, your network will determine your net worth, and influence is as powerful as capital when it comes to building wealth. If you meet someone with the capacity to help you in your journey or expand your sphere of influence, be sure to have quality questions ready to ask. Many wealthy and influential people want to help others, but only when they see their contribution is reciprocal, beneficial and appreciated. (Go to www.RickHale.com for a list of interview questions to consider in advance of a strategic meeting.)

If getting referrals and building business relationships is part of your mission, consider reading an excellent book by my good friend Michael J. Maher, *The 7 L's of Communication*. He provides valuable insights about creating intentional connections with influencers. Michael shares his performance mantra: "'Each and every day, someone, somewhere in my city, needs my services. My job TODAY is to find that person.' Internalize this and you'll think like a top producer."[20]

QUESTIONS TO CONSIDER:

1. In what ways do you think your current circle or sphere of influence needs to be improved? What changes need to occur immediately? Which are more long-term?

2. Which of the twenty-four areas for building your influence sounded like the best place(s) to start for you? What other locations did you think of?

3. As you start to make better connections, what are three things you can offer others in exchange for the expertise they bring to the relationship?

4. Which of the twenty-five tips for networking in a group setting most appealed to you? How can you apply those ideas to your specific business or organization?

5. Do you already have an impressive elevator speech? If not, craft one now and start practicing it until you're ready to deliver it on a moment's notice. It needs to be clear, concise and memorable!

CHAPTER 10

WEALTH BUILDING

Wealth building is a fascinating topic, one that's simple in theory but difficult to attain . . . and even harder to sustain. You've probably heard the statistic that many lottery winners quickly go from multimillionaires to near poverty simply because the money alone doesn't make them sustainably rich, and in fact, often it leads to impulsive, poor choices and behaviors. A 2017 study by Brandon Gaille found that 70% of all lottery winners end up broke and filing bankruptcy, 1% file bankruptcy each year, only 55% of those polled who won the lottery felt their lives were better and they were happier, and 43% actually said their winnings made no impact on happiness at all.[21] So . . . shed the belief that fast wealth always brings happiness! Being wealthy is a holistic experience; keeping financial benefits—whether earned, inherited or won—is based on wise financial habits, a proper mindset for investing and the preservation of wealth. Remaining wealthy is a learned skill just like earning and investing.

In a fascinating 2019 report, the consulting firm Cerulli Associates projected that over the next quarter century, roughly 45 million U.S. households will collectively bequeath over $68 trillion to their heirs. This constitutes the largest redistribution of wealth in human history. Generation X stands to inherit 57% of that amount, and millennials the bulk of the balance.[22] Each generation forms its own collective opinion on social constructs and values, which then shapes their collective future. Infusing massive amounts of capital into the mix in the form of inheritance is like pouring gasoline on the cultural fire, especially since many millennials value experiences more than things. My friends and I have had an up close look at the values of millennials, and we're eager (and a bit anxious) about how they'll handle the influx of inherited wealth.

I've observed that those who earn wealth often treat it differently than those who inherit or win it. Those who have survived the ups and downs of accumulation over time often learn important lessons and fail forward, they experience more pride and fulfillment, and they are typically wiser in how they handle money. Perhaps lottery winners often lose so much of it because they didn't earn it the old fashion way, nor did they learn the lessons around money acquisition and preservation or find role models to emulate and give them wise counsel. They may even suffer from the "imposter syndrome"—in their hearts, they don't believe they deserve it, so they experience insecurity and self-doubt, knowing they didn't develop the high-level business skills of those who have earned their wealth. But all of us can be afflicted by this syndrome and undermine their own success subconsciously and struggle to truly enjoy and embrace it. I have friends who have earned every penny they have and earned significant wealth but still battle with self-doubt because when they were young, they absorbed messages that they would never be good enough or have enough. In some cases, peers may also impact a wealthy person's perspective on self-worth because they treat him as second-class, unworthy, and still an outsider. This is sometimes framed as "old rich" snobbery over the "new rich."

A problem that's far more common than sudden wealth is generational poverty. Some of us have grown up barely scraping by, and the struggle has had enormous consequences on our identity and confidence. In economics, a "poverty trap" is caused by self-reinforcing mechanisms that cause poverty to persist unless there is outside intervention. In developing countries, it's known as the "development trap." Some people who suffer in these environments never develop the capacity to perform the most basic functions of saving, spending wisely, and investing. Many others have climbed out of poverty and found relative security, but they still live with the lingering fear of sliding back into that deep, dark hole. The best way to combat this stigma is through coaching, positive role models and some version of professional counseling that provides honest and affirming feedback. In a safe and positive relationship, people can face their fears, overcome their doubts, and chart a more productive course. Our perspective (on life, purpose, relationships, work, family, and everything else that's important to us) is the product of our relationships. Like sponges, we absorb either confidence or fear from the air we breathe when we're with people. It's important, then, to take stock of our connections: Who are those, past or present, who make us feel incompetent, and who are those, past and present, who inspire us? Do we need to make some hard decisions to limit our involvement with toxic people and spend more time with those who will have a more positive effect? (In case you're wondering, the answer for almost all of us is "Yes!") Make it a priority to spend time with wise, mature, gifted people who care enough about you to enter your world and bring out the best in you. Soon, you'll develop a powerful blend of humility and boldness—knowing that you don't have all the answers, but confident that you have what it takes to move forward. You'll be a better listener, you'll make better decisions, and your stress level will go way down. None of this happens, though, if we aren't honest about our struggles and if we don't find someone to coach us.

Your greatest asset is yourself. Invest in developing your body, mind, spirit, and skills. As you learn and grow, your love for people will be more evident, and you'll sharpen your professional talents. I believe it's more important to invest in ourselves than in any fund or business venture. When we do that, we'll experience wealth in many different dimensions.

A holistic definition of wealth is critical for you to learn and grow. If you can clearly define an awesome life and stay on the path to your goals, you'll always feel the power of progress and personal potential. That's the elixir for insecurity, lack of purpose and the imposter syndrome. Gradually, confidence will replace insecurity, and gratitude will replace fear. You'll learn to appreciate who you are, as well as who you are becoming. Perfectionism cripples our souls, but progress reinforces hope. My goal is to give you confidence to become your best self. Nothing less than that.

I would encourage you to think big. Why not create a bucket list without limitations? Wealth isn't worth much if it's hoarded. It should be used with wisdom and creativity to enrich the lives of those we love. To expand your mind and heart, look at sample bucket lists. For instance, here are ten ideas for travel:

1. Swim in each of the four major oceans

2. Visit at least three out of the seven new Wonders of the World

3. Touch six out of the seven continents (Antarctica is optional!)

4. Journey to the Grand Canyon

5. Road trip across the entire United States

6. Go on a week-long cruise

7. Experience the Northern Lights

8. Dive at the Great Barrier Reef

9. Hike through the Himalayas

10. Go on a wildlife safari[23]

Let's come back to the basics: A good, working definition of wealth is difficult for many people to get their arms around, so let's start with that challenge.

WHAT'S YOUR DEFINITION OF WEALTH?

It's not merely a certain amount of money in the bank or an investment portfolio. The path to wealth is about far more than money. A life worth living is hitting your goals in all quadrants and the spokes represented on the Life Wheel, constantly striving to improve yourself in each category. To come up with your definition, you need more than an off-handed, quick review. It requires careful analysis, good planning, and tenacious execution. Without these elements, you're like a rudderless boat on a stormy sea.

MY DEFINITION

Here's my personal definition of wealth: Wealth is having the capacity to make key choices without fear of disrupting your life plan, stability and well-being. It's having enough so any setback won't be significantly detrimental to your family. This wealth isn't tied to a particular job or someone else's demands—it's independent enough to always support your values and mission. It's doing what you really want to do without a loan or loading up credit cards that create debt-fueled stress. This kind of wealth gives you the capacity to be fearlessly generous when someone has a need. Sacrificing for others is both challenging and fulfilling, but when you're financially insecure, it's human nature to hold on to everything you have, which prevents you from experiencing the joy of generosity. Real wealth aligned with a generous heart is a big, full life.

Another benefit of wealth is that you can trade money for time, and you can use that time to help others. True wealth includes the capacity to leave a financial mark on the world. You may choose to spread your contributions, or you may pick one or a few to have a bigger impact on them. The best organizations have rigorous financial systems to be sure most of the money goes to those in need, rather than for administration and fundraising.

Bob Kilinski, a lifelong mentor and an amazing human being, teaches a wealth-building workshop for agents in our company. His definition of a wealthy person is simply having one dollar more in consistent and continuous passive income than it takes to fund your chosen life. He would add that it also requires an emergency fund for life's speed bumps and unexpected detours. His teaching has significantly shaped my strategies for building and sustaining wealth, and I've learned many lessons included in this chapter that will lead to winning with your finances.

To be sure, I can't teach you everything I've learned in building sustainable wealth, and you'll find plenty of tips and tricks in mainstream media and books, but hopefully, my insights will inspire a subtle shift in how you approach wealth, and you'll be thirsty to learn more.

CRUCIAL STEPS

Step 1

The first step toward a wealthy life is developing a positive mindset. Some people grow up with parents who impart this perspective, but the rest of us have to find ways to acquire it. Changing the script of your mindset may take serious work that includes coaching, skill building, developing new habits and counseling to replace ingrained negative perspectives about money. But it's always about far more than money— your self-worth and your future impact hang in the balance. Breaking the cycle of poverty or mediocrity is a massive challenge. But when you do, it's a huge personal triumph, one that will impact generations to come. Don't forget to consider all twelve categories in the Life Wheel. Money is a factor in all of them.

Step 2

Step two is creating a sound, workable budget and setting SMART goals. Some people are naturally detailed and specific in handling money, but they're often married to someone who isn't! It's important then, for all the decision makers to have input, with plenty of give and take, so the budget is clear and honored by everyone involved.

Step 3

Step three is to know the rules of money while keeping an open mind about building a wealth platform. This includes seeking wise counsel to assist you. Here are some basic laws of personal money management:

1. As a rule, pay cash or cash equivalent whenever possible, and don't carry credit card debt. All credit card debt should be paid off monthly unless the interest rate is below that of a predictably safe investment (this is so rare that it's practically nonexistent) or you're in an emergency.

2. Purchase protection in the form of insurance, including adequate life, home and property insurance, disability, as well as insurance for your vehicle. Protect your assets, especially yourself, your greatest asset.

3. Create and update a budget and follow it—avoid impulse buying.

4. Save for purchases and avoid debt on consumables, non-appreciating assets and toys. Live beneath your means.

5. Buy based on *needs* first and *wants* second, and only within your budget.

6. Think *repair* first and *replace* second when things break or wear out. Think *new* last. As an example, you probably don't need a new iPhone or computer every year if your current one is working, even if Apple ads tell you otherwise.

7. In a commission- or personal-based business, pay yourself first, not last.

8. Gladly tithe and give regularly to noble causes that align with your heart.

9. Invest regularly, following a balanced investment strategy that aligns with your risk tolerance, personal needs and desired financial future.

10. Save and invest no less than 20% of your personal income for retirement. One simple formula is to live off 70% or less of your personal income, invest 10%, save 10% (that's the 20% for retirement) and tithe or donate 10% to causes you support.

COMMON MISTAKES

Here's a list of mistakes people often make regarding money:

1. Having a consumptive lifestyle with little emphasis on saving and investing.

2. Having no financial goals.

3. Failing to get out and stay out of debt.

4. Not having a workable personal budget—or failing to contemplate one for the future as life circumstances evolve.

5. Failing to save for emergencies (six months minimum in liquid assets).

6. Buying new cars and oversized, expensive houses too soon, solely for ego purposes.

7. Buying things in anticipation of money yet to be realized.

8. Spending money as a tax reduction or deduction as the sole rationale.

9. Believing that saving equals investing.

10. Failing to start investing early and enjoying the benefits of compounded returns.

11. Asking "Should I invest or not?" instead of "Where should I invest?"

12. Not balancing your portfolio and not taking into account the reality of risk vs reward as the economic outlook shifts.

13. Investing without a clear understanding of whether you're in accumulation mode or preservation mode in your age and stage of life.

14. Failing to follow the proper and sequential investment strategies.

15. Not saving for major purchases and incurring debt to buy them.

16. Allowing expensive debt to fund consumables and depreciating assets.

17. Failing to have a monthly plan to contribute a percentage or fixed amount toward savings and investing.

When you spend more money than you have, you're headed for big trouble. Whether you are in a commission-based, salaried, or hourly job, a budget will clarify your income and outflow of money. I'm stunned by how few people have a written budget including basic monthly expenses like housing, food, gas, investing and savings, and of course, consumables and fun. Your budget should include a comfortable margin for investing, or for those who are no longer working, for security on a fixed income. If you're prone to outspend your budget because you use credit cards, move to a cash-based system like the one created by Dave Ramsay. (Information can be found in his books and online resources at www.ramsaysolutions.com.)

INVESTING

The only debt I recommend is one that leverages the acquisition of appreciating, tax-advantaged investments. It's also smart to have diversity in your investments that allows for liquidity in times of economic uncertainty or short-term opportunities when you need cash quickly.

If you borrow at a 4% interest rate and have a guaranteed return of 8% or more, that makes sense, and you win! You've used O.P.P (Other People's Money) for a good return, and that's brilliant. This is especially true if your investment is tied to income-producing real estate. They aren't making more of it, so supply and demand favor investments in real estate, especially if it's held long term. Why not create a real estate portfolio that pays for itself in monthly income but also covers the debt and principal paydown? This concept seems intuitively obvious, but I'm always surprised by how often people buy expensive six-figure cars or other luxuries with bank loans and high interest credit cards instead of investing that money in appreciating, income-producing assets. They then play catch up for their entire lives, living paycheck to paycheck, trapped in that cycle while they hope someone or something will miraculously show up and save the day (like winning the lottery, a big inheritance, or Social Security). The only thing worse than fear is false hope. Get real! Why not delay gratification, create a plan for wealth building, and one day allow residual gains from those investments to pay for the luxuries in cash or from the gain on the principal? It sounds easy, but it's not. All of us are trained by our culture as professional consumers who often make poor choices, but it doesn't have to be that way—it's your choice.

My first taste of investing came at the age of twenty-five. I was single and saw a house for sale at what appeared to be a great price. Like most of my peers, I didn't have great role models of wealth-building habits, and saving money wasn't natural for me, but I knew one thing: I was paying rent that was going toward someone else's mortgage each month, and it was better to own than rent. So I went to my grandmother and asked, "Is there any way you would advance me $10,000 to buy a house?" I promised to pay her back when I sold it, if not sooner. The down payment was more than that, so I used a loan against my 401k to make up the difference. This money was borrowed at a very low interest rate. (I later paid it back to preserve the sanctity of the rules in a retirement account.) This was a very effective leveraging strategy you should consider when you're ready to buy. If you don't have the capacity to borrow from family members for a first-time down payment, you can save for it. And if you're truly entrepreneurial, find a great investment property and partner with someone with money for the down payment and credentials for a loan. You can oversee any needed renovations, manage renters and make the partnership successful. Then, over time you can bank the monthly profits and combine it with gains from that first shared investment into one of your own as the sole investor and owner.

For my first house, the monthly payments were approximately $1,150 per month, so I rented out rooms to three of my buddies. Each renter paid me $350 per month, so I was able to live in a decent house for only about $200 per month personally, the balance of the mortgage, insurance and principal. We of course split utilities. I didn't have a term for it then, but this is now called "house hacking." It's when you buy a home and rent rooms to offset the carrying costs of your portion of a home, and it's brilliant! You could even create a small apartment in a basement or attic that becomes a source of income to offset the carrying costs. In fact, my friend Craig Curelop has written a book called *House Hacking*. Pick it up. You'll learn a lot.

Talk about being excited and proud! I knew I was making an investment every time I wrote that mortgage check. No more renting. No more throwing money out the window each month. I was paying far less than any rent in the Atlanta area while simultaneously owning a great little house. In addition to the joy of home ownership, I was also getting back about $2,500 in cash value via tax benefits each year because I was deducting the interest I paid on the house. But the icing on the cake came when I sold the home four years later for net $30,000 more than what I had paid. I decided right then that this type of investing was for me. And as the tax code exists today, you can earn up to $250,000 individually or $500,000 as a married couple *tax free*! My $30,000 gain was really equivalent to over $40,000 in value when you factor the tax advantages. At the time, this was almost equal to a year's net income after taxes from my job, and without any added workload!

After I repaid my grandmother, I used the rest of the money as a down payment on my next home. This was more than seed money; it was a seed planted in my life—the seed of wealth building. I was officially an investor, and I never looked back. Three houses later, it was obvious that with each successful purchase and sale, my credit rating improved, and my down payment capacity also had grown by netting compounded profits with each sale. Both of those factors, along with a consistent "on-time" payment history, earned me the right to preferred interest rates on future properties. Another secret to wealth building is to pay less in interest so you'll have more to invest over time. Banks like real estate-hedged collateral for other business and home investments that produce compounding returns.

Over the next few years, I bought and flipped a few houses. Most of those projects did well. Some did extremely well. I purchased rental properties and invested in three commercial buildings. The only time I ever lost money on was a development project right before the market crash in 2007. Even that one would have been profitable if I hadn't had to sell out mid-crash and take a loss due to partnerships and external financial needs. This painful experience proved to be a classroom for me. A quality, real-world education can be expensive, but it's invaluable as you mature as an investor with a mind for building wealth. You often learn a lot more from failures than successes.

It's quite rare that people lose money in real estate especially long term. Those who do typically just sell at the wrong time out of necessity and personal circumstances when cash crunched due to a personal situation or market shift. If I had held on to my first home, it would be worth about $600,000 today (purchased for $153,000), almost quadruple the original purchase price in the early 90's, so know that it's not necessary to hold real estate for thirty years but if you do, even simply paying off the mortgage over time will create an economic windfall in the end. Truth is, in many markets, it's not uncommon to be able to sell at a profit within five or ten years and roll investments into other opportunities if the current one has limitations. Imagine having 10, 15 or 25 homes you buy over time, rent out and pay off over 20 to 30 years. Your income would be far greater than the benefits you'd realize from Social Security. Couple that with a little luck in the form of appreciation, and the portfolio starts to look amazing!

I'm also a fan of automated investing from each paycheck before the funds hit my bank account. I do this with my 401k and IRA, and also for life insurance that guarantees my debt is fully covered if I die early. It would also provide sufficient cash flow for my wife to live comfortably for the rest of her life. That provides real peace of mind.

WEALTH BUILDING—AND THE LOSS OF IT—
OFTEN HAPPENS SLOWLY . . .
THEN SUDDENLY.

My conclusion: be careful to establish habits that favor the best possible outcome for your money and investing.

THE NECESSARY REQUIREMENTS

You've been taking steps to create an expanding and reliable network. At the same time, you should be using that network to build an ever-expanding portfolio of investments. Your goal now is to be growing your available cash and influence. My avenue for doing this at first was in real estate sales, but there are many great jobs and opportunities that can fund passive investments. I saw no other pursuit that would provide $30,000 of cash in three years, so I worked to put

WEALTH BUILDING | 223

my money to work early. I maxed out a savings strategy and also my 401(k) and found real estate deals that suited me using those as a source for down payments. Today, I also use my stock portfolio and whole life insurance policies as borrowing power for appreciating assets and investments. Notice, I didn't say "to buy expensive toys . . . cars, boats, and vacation homes with loans." When the bank uses my secure assets, I receive the lowest interest rates because of the low risk. An insightful book on building and transferring wealth with insurance is by Garrett Gunderson: *What Would the Rockefellers Do: How the wealthy get and stay that way, and you can too.*

The "big four" tools you need to grow wealth are *cash*, *credit*, *expertise*, and *influence*. I knew that if I didn't have those requirements, I would never be invited to the table for bigger investment opportunities.

There are numerous ways to acquire these tools. If you simply bought a house to rent each year for two years, you could build your credit, increase your expertise in rental properties, and develop relationships where people trust you and will allow you to buy bigger properties. You'll find an infinite number of ways to increase your value in those four categories if you apply some creativity and hustle. And if you're really entrepreneurial and savvy in business, you might compound your investment strategy by taking on investors to fund additions to your portfolio (flips and holds for the long haul). Although you'd have to share in the profits and proceeds from the first day, their capital might allow you to fast track a bigger portfolio. It's often better to have a smaller piece of a much larger pie. This form of investing is a quick way to scale your enterprise and leads to significant long-term wealth creation. But the key to winning with syndications with investors is to create a sterling reputation as a professional with a track record of a winning strategy. (My friend Michael Blank offers a course on how to syndicate when buying apartments and investment properties. You can find his podcasts and print material at themichaelblank.com. I'd also recommend the "Bigger Pockets Podcast" for additional education and inspiration on investing in real estate and other opportunities.)

I often ask myself, "If it's to be, then why not me?" And why not you? You've made it this far in the book, so you're clearly motivated and I'm assuming you have a good work ethic. That's what it takes to become a great wealth builder as you continually improve your standing in the "big six" areas.

1. A commission- or bonus-based career with tremendous upside financially when you perform above the standard.

2. Establishing a budget and financial goals, updated each year.

3. Real estate investments: personal home, rental homes, commercial properties, and syndications in larger real estate projects.

4. Business ownership: My role in the real estate sector opens doors in many areas, and my actual real estate team is a business all its own. You can own your own businesses and invest in other people's businesses too.

5. Retirement savings and investments (mutual funds, stocks and bonds, etc.) which are automated and paid out monthly per your plan.

6. Life and health insurance to guarantee my family's future with ongoing financial stability.

Two outstanding books written by Robert Kyosaki, *Cash Flow Quadrant* and *Rich Dad Poor Dad*, changed the way I've built wealth. Real wealth comes from passive income attached to appreciating assets you can improve and that pay for themselves over time. Magic lives on the right side of Kyosaki's Cash Flow Quadrant! Here's what the quadrants looks like:

Employee / Job	Business Ownership
Self-Employed	Investments

The Employee/Job quadrant is 100% dependent on an employer's desire and ability to pay you. Self-Employed can be lucrative and good source of cash flow if you provide a valuable service and you're a quality marketer and/or salesperson. But where things get really interesting and fun is when you move a sales opportunity or service industry into the Business Ownership box (investing in your own company or investing in other owner/operators businesses). The magic in a successful business is that you are typically leveraging other people for support, tech and manufacturing, and also inspiring salespeople to magnify returns you can't get doing it alone.

The fourth quadrant is Investments. Anyone can strategically win in this box over time by pushing income and savings into investment accounts that hold stocks, bonds and passive real estate investments. If you actively build and manage a rental portfolio, that's a Business Ownership box . . . and a profitable side business! Look at the quadrants: Where does your income come from and where do your assets live?

Fast forward to today, 30 years after my first home purchase and establishing and funding of my first 401(k) many things have sprouted and grown. With the help of my initial real estate connections, I now own six commercial properties. (Technically, I *partially* own them because I choose to partner with people who bring specific skills and influence to the table.) I have partial ownership in twelve Keller Williams offices, a real estate sales team, an interest in a real estate holding company, an insurance company and a vintage guitar store. Over time I've also invested in numerous real estate acquisitions, including over ten real estate syndications. Note: once you have a million dollars in assets, not counting your primary residence, you can invest in other offerings that are bigger than your capacity as an accredited investor. Examples are investing with twenty or more investors in a large commercial office building, medical complex or a 250-unit apartment building. The operator acquires, renovates and manages each project, making it 100% passive in terms of time and energy on the part of the investors. It's wise to benefit from other people's core genius and expertise, and sometimes, bigger projects have more capacity to survive dips in the market if managed properly.

The key to investing with others is to carefully consider the character, business savvy and experience of the operator and his/her team. Don't make assumptions, and if the promised financial returns seem extraordinarily high, pay even closer attention because quality operators don't have to overpay to win investors. Most of the time, a syndication's rate of return is lower than finding, buying and managing them yourself, but it's easier, and success is more predictable if you carefully choose the right operators. If you have that expertise, you can find the deal and support the management, and others like me will fund them for you and share the financial rewards. None of this would have been possible without initially borrowing some money from my grandmother and taking the risk to buy a property. I had to start somewhere, and I was committed to building wealth from the beginning.

Your journey awaits, and you simply need to start (or start over again) to expand your financial future to ensure you can fund the life you envision for yourself. Passive income is the only way to be sure you can have and do what you want, when you want, regardless of the situation you face. If your sole income depends on your ability to show up for work every day to earn a living, financial trouble is only one health crisis away.

Once you have enough passive income plus liquid reserves (cash or equivalent) for emergencies, by definition you're wealthy! But remember, for this to work consistently, you have to stay on top of your expenses and budget for the lifestyle you want. With your commitment to those figures now and in the future, you can reverse engineer the amount of passive income you need to fulfill the goal of true freedom and a life worth living . . . and one day leave an amazing legacy.

THE ALLURE OF REAL ESTATE SALES AS A CAREER OPTION

During my first year in the real estate sales industry, I noticed an interesting trend. Most of my friends were single and fast approaching (or just past) thirty years old. By then, many were on the hunt for the perfect mate. That year I sold houses or condos to approximately ten single females, and by the following year, most of them had found a special someone, and many were engaged. Coincidence? I don't think so. Since then, I've confirmed that home ownership improves self-esteem, and a healthy balance sheet increases a person's attractiveness.

Instinctively, most of us are attracted to success and successful people. It's that simple. Everyone suffers occasional setbacks, but those who have developed a can-do spirit and never-quit mindset are the ones who will be winners in the end.

Owning real estate has many advantages. Below are some of the primary ones.

1. *Leverage.* You only need to put a small amount down to buy a home, but you immediately gain asset value appreciation on the total value. So if you make a down payment of $10,000 on a $100,000 home, and the home goes up $10,000 in value, you've already enjoyed a 100 percent return on your cash in! In contrast, if you buy stocks, you have to invest 100 percent of the value to get the return . . . and stocks are often far more volatile.

2. *Mortgage interest is tax deductible.* In some cases, it's like Uncle Sam paying for a couple months' mortgage payments for you every year. For example, if you paid $9,000 in interest (which is front-loaded and highest during the first few years of a mortgage loan) and are in the thirty percent tax bracket, you reduce your taxable income by the $9,000. It equates to a true cash value of $3,000.

3. *Appreciation potential.* The housing market typically appreciates in value over the long run. During tougher times, like an economic recession, the downside is less extreme.

4. *Pride in home ownership.* The value of something usually varies depending on supply and demand. But when it comes to land, the current supply is all we'll ever have. Being able to buy property, own it, and have the right to will it to your heirs is a special privilege. Supply never increases, but as long as demand exists, you will come out ahead over time.

5. *No tax on capital gains on the sale of a property.* To qualify for this benefit at the time of this writing, you must live on the property for two of five years prior to selling as the owner/occupant.

The limits are $250,000 for an individual and $500,000 in non-taxable gains for a married couple. That means if you make $50,000 in appreciation when you sell, and if you lived there two of five years, you get to keep 100 percent of the money. At the thirty percent tax bracket, that's equivalent to making over $70,000 more than if you had made the same amount at a traditional job for which you would be taxed.

6. *You can defer certain capital gains taxes with a "1031 exchange."* As stated in IRS code Section 1031, property owners can swap one commercial or like-kind property for another, if not "owner occupied," with no or limited tax due at the exchange. You'd only do that with a property you hadn't lived in for two of five years as a primary residence. Be sure to consult an expert in this area in advance of selling and exchanging like-kind properties to ensure you qualify, and apply the proper rules to the transaction for IRS compliance purposes.

7. *Forced savings.* Buying a home is a form of savings. After you pay off your mortgage, the asset is yours. You'd have to pay rent anyway, so why not pay off a home and end up with a valuable asset you can apply to your retirement? A further incentive is that if you pay one extra payment each December from year one of a thirty-year loan, you can reduce your mortgage time significantly. How much you save depends on the interest rate, of course, but a 13th payment each year on a $200,000 loan at five percent interest reduces the payment period from thirty to twenty-six years, saving $32,000 in interest! You can collateralize a loan, refinance later, or utilize reverse mortgage for cash flow when you slow down and move toward retirement. Here's a link to a helpful mortgage payment calculator: http://www.

bankrate.com/calculators/home-equity/additional-mortgage-payment-calculator.aspx.

8. *You start to build your bank credibility.* Many Americans hope to start their own business one day and may need a bank loan to support the endeavor. The first thing banks look for is great credit and your personal financial statement (along with debt-to-income ratios and other specifics). A record of buying investment real estate with a solid repayment history is a big step in the right direction!

9. *Build a real estate portfolio.* Expand your retirement plan with rental properties. Buying ten homes and paying them off over a thirty-year span virtually guarantees a million-dollar or better portfolio.

10. *Buying a home tends to elevate your self-esteem and social credibility.* I can't guarantee it in your case, but few deny that people are generally attracted to success. Test this theory yourself. It's not much of a reach to assume owning a home could improve self-confidence and also enhance your dating résumé if you're still single! It's a least a good conversation starter. Start building wealth and see who shows up! If nothing else, it's just smart to invest in real estate.

PITFALLS TO AVOID IF REAL ESTATE SALES IS A CAREER CHOICE (OR ANY OTHER SALES CAREER OR IN ANY SMALL BUSINESS YOU MIGHT START)

Remember, you can build wealth in real estate as a strong portion of your portfolio without making real estate your career. Many do, and the advantage is avoiding licensing requirements, education, and compliance that goes with the proper licensing in the United States. If you choose to pursue real estate as an investment, I highly recommend reading as many books on the topic as you can and hiring a professional skilled at handling the process of vetting options and negotiating the best properties for your goals, budget, and needs, including single-family and multi-family homes, as well as commercial buildings and land. I recommended *The Millionaire Real Estate Investor*, *Flip*, and *Hold*, all coauthored by Gary Keller, and *Wealth Can't Wait* by David Osborn. Also visit Bigger Pockets (www.biggerpockets.com), the website for real estate investors with tools, resources, podcasts, and other resources. If you choose to make real estate sales a career choice, be careful choosing the company you work for. Who you're in business with and the value the relationship brings really matters. I've had a tremendous experience with Keller Williams Realty and am loyal to the core. Do your homework in your local market to make an intelligent decision about which company fits you best. Consider company culture, tools and resources, education, hands-on coaching, and accountability.

Yet I don't want to be accused of misleading you. I've had financial success thanks to my career in real estate, and more importantly, I've loved every minute of it. But that doesn't mean it's been a walk in the park for me . . . and it won't be for you. You're bound to deal with several pitfalls along the way. If you can avoid some of them, good for you! If not, you learn to power through. Below are some potential pitfalls to watch for while becoming a wealth builder.

Unbelief

When I teach classes to new real estate professionals, I encourage them to set a financial goal, even if it's their first year in the industry. For some reason, new agents often choose a goal to earn $100,000. I don't know what it is about that number, but men, women, young, and old declare confidently in class, "I will earn $100,000 in commission this year!" They appear strong and sure that day.

However, I've seen what happens not long after the class. For some, doubt begins to creep in on the car ride home. For others, it shows up when their cold calls don't warm up. A few make it several weeks without a listing or seeing the stream of eager buyers they imagined while the ink was drying on their newly minted real estate licenses before they quietly decide to settle for lesser goals or quit. Seventy-five percent of the people in our industry quit within the first two years of licensing. In real estate and every other profession, I would imagine even more than that give up on their big goals after a few failed attempts.

Whatever your financial and wealth-building goals, the first step is to imagine yourself with the goal in hand. You must feel it, see it, and believe it with every fiber of your being. By definition, a goal is a high-level achievement that won't necessarily be easy or immediate. You need to prepare to stick with it for the long haul. You must know *why* you want to earn $100,000 . . . save $40,000 . . . close twenty transactions . . . sell a million-dollar home . . . or whatever you've determined to do. Without a strong *why*, you're sure to become a victim of unbelief.

Your internal belief-o-meter must be set to succeed. Like a thermostat in your home, your belief-o-meter always does what it's programmed to do. If your thermostat is set to 65 degrees, it won't stop trying to get there. You may forget to close some windows on a hot day when you turn on the air conditioner. You may be cooking on your stovetop all day, or using the fireplace, but eventually the thermostat will get the house to 65 degrees. That's its job!

If your belief-o-meter is set to $100,000, you'll get there, regardless of a slow start or soft market. You'll outlast the difficulties. And if your belief-o-meter is set to $50,000, you may begin to close more deals and build momentum, but your sales won't rise far beyond that amount.

My good friend Eeman Heisler entered the real estate industry a few years ago, and very soon, her work ethic and tenacious approach to serving people led her to great success. She had left the dental industry and was now fully committed to her role in real estate. She didn't have a backup plan—no back door, no second choices . . . winning was her only option. She credits much of her success to her extraordinary level of commitment: working sixty-hour weeks, fielding hundreds of calls, posting inspiring and funny messages on social media, and pursuing lead-generation or incoming calls from prospects who might become a client and result in a transaction. She now recruits and coaches future stars in sales. She will tell you what she did is repeatable, but nothing is more important than locking in an early success. It's the moment you stop *hoping* you can and realize you can actually do it! You have to find your "I believe" moment and build on it! Define it, reach for it, and get a coach and an accountability partner to ensure you make that mark. That "belief check box" that is on everyone's list of life goals simply implies that the moment you *know* you can, your level of commitment and belief in yourself skyrockets and you start attaining your goals! This story is about real estate as a career, but it applies to any endeavor where self-doubt is a major obstacle. Do you really believe it's possible? And what does the path look like?

Begin to build wealth by visualizing it. If you can't visualize, you will be resigned to a defeated attitude because somewhere inside you, you are saying, "I don't deserve it," or "I can't do it." But you *do* deserve it! You *can* do this! Jack Canfield in his book The Success Principles speaks to a concept called becoming an Inverse Paranoid. That concept supports the idea that the world wants what is best for you in all situations. Not that all situations are amazing and perfect, but that it's part of the journey and to your advantage and benefit even it produces a failing moment or experience, the education will make you wiser and more capable as more opportunities present themselves. It's the opposite of being paranoid where the world is conspiring against you and contradicts Murphy's Law where any and everything that can go wrong will go wrong. The issue with being over cautious and chronically pessimistic is that you won't try or take any chances and that will lead to stagnation. Stagnation will never support your leveling up. Seek Coaches, consultants, models and systems that are proven for sure, and don't foolishly rush into every opportunity, but by taking strategic risks you'll learn and win more often. Then the secret is to not quit! Keep amending your path and decision making chain with each experience good or bad and keep swinging! What if you try 9 times and quit and it's the 10th try that produces a huge win? If it works for other folks, it'll likely work for you at some point. Model winning behavior, don't give up, and you'll become a winner with winning results to be proud of.

It's important to realize what got you *here* might not get you *there*. In *Wealth Made Easy,* Gary S. Reid and Gary M. Krebs list many hacks to creating wealth. They mention the spider monkey's demise in Wealth Hack #25. The South American spider monkey is sought after by hunters, but it's not an easy catch . . . except for one thing. They are very curious and not terribly smart. The flaw of the spider monkey is their basic instinct of "holding your nuts" at all costs. Reid and Krebs explain that to catch spider monkeys, the simple trick is to put a large nut inside a heavy container with a hole just big enough for their hand to fit into it. They're curious by design and love nuts. When they reach into the hole and grab the nut, they get stuck, but they're so stubborn they refuse to let go. They could easily be freed by letting go of the nut, but they become victims of their own tight grip.[24]

This metaphor represents many of our innate habits to hold onto one thing because we "have it in hand already," but we eliminate the option for something better. If you want different, better or more, you have to release what you currently have.

Why do some people win big and others struggle? Here are a few common pitfalls to consider:

Inconsistent Work Ethic

When I was starting out, I was willing to work ten-, twelve-, or fourteen-hour days. That's how I built a database of people who trusted me and also showed enough homes that lead to contracts and ultimately commission from closings. I knew I couldn't network my way to success if I didn't follow through. I couldn't be an asset in the lives of others if I didn't work hard to deliver what I promised and I had to be available when they were to ensure they succeeded.

Although the payoff of hard work seems obvious in commissioned-based sales, this attitude also works in every career. Simply put, stand out from the pack—it pays to out-produce and overachieve if you want to earn bigger opportunities through promotions. Make a difference in the lives of those around you by bringing your most productive and positive self, and watch the response. But be careful not to alienate those around you. I assure you that if you hustle and they don't, they'll resent you. Be thoughtful and kind, but to move ahead, you'll have to outperform others and ignore the pressure from small thinkers along the way.

The first step in that process is self-mastery and expertise. In my business, not unlike many in sales and service-oriented businesses, I couldn't rely on one big client. I wouldn't want to, even if that were possible. For me, it is the relational spider web that fuels every part of my success. I must be disciplined enough to forge relationships with people who see me as part of their success. If I ever bring a product to the table that is below standards, that web breaks. If my expertise delivers anything short of a stellar experience, I'm dead. There's always someone in the wings ready to displace me. And in the immortal words of Ricky Bobby from the movie *Talladega Nights*, "You're either first or last. Second place is the first loser." Each win will lead to more wins in sales and referrals!

Without a consistent work ethic and intense focus on high standards, the network does nothing for me. I would just build a network of people who think I am haphazard and sloppy. So networking and work ethic go hand in hand. You need a strong commitment to grow your network, and you also need the consistent work ethic to ensure that network believes in you.

It takes time and commitment just to get started, but anyone can work from 6 a.m. to 10 p.m., just trying to connect with as many people as possible. But your network isn't going to include everyone. You don't have the time or bandwidth to pour into everyone, so you need discipline to identify and commit to the right twenty percent of your contacts. You are looking for the twenty percent who will yield the best results for your business, and then you invest your time into building connections with those people. Sure, you have to kiss a lot of frogs to find a prince, but don't just walk out to the pond every day and start kissing. Not every frog is equal.

For example, some people buy a house once and live in it for thirty years. They have a great experience with my team, but they never refer us. I'm appreciative and happy to do business with those people, but I'm not going to expend the same amount of relational energy on them as a repeat client that buys, sells or invests in real estate every 2 to 4 years that also refers business regularly from their sphere. I'm looking for people who are connectors, who are magnets, who are influencers. I'm looking for those who refer business to me regularly because they see value in my ability to provide quality service to them, their family, friends and coworkers. That inner circle of "wealth determiners" is my twenty percent.

Please don't misunderstand me. Of course, all people are equal in God's eyes. Certainly, every life is important. However, not every businessperson is equal in terms of your business success. You need to find the twenty percent of people who can most influence the outcome of your business, and that requires laser focus and consistent work on your part to keep from spending your time unwisely.

Are you spending time developing the wrong group of people? Ask yourself on a regular basis, "Am I watering the weeds?" It takes consistent focus to keep from wasting time. Discipline yourself to spend the right amount of time with the right people for the right reason.

Also ask yourself, "Who needs to know you?" I must admit that the answer to this question isn't always obvious. It requires staying open and alert to potential opportunities. It also means illustrating your best capacity to serve above the standard in your industry every day, whoever is in front of you. And if opportunity knocks, open the door!

As an example, in 2003, my office got a call from a man who said his name was Ralph. He wanted to see a property of mine. Paula, a professional working in my office, explained that I was on vacation and that she would have another agent from our team show him the property as soon as he was available. He told her that he would wait for me to return and wanted to meet with me personally. However, before he hung up, he quizzed her about the market and our team structure.

That seemed off to Paula, so she called me on vacation, which she rarely did because she knew that we all need quality time away from work! But this situation was unique. Ralph asked questions most people don't, which raised her curiosity. She thought I should call him even though he was adamant about me calling after I returned. Typically, a buyer generally wants to see a property as soon as possible and isn't concerned about which agent opens the door. I agreed that this sounded odd, so I called Ralph back immediately. He asked a variety of strange questions, but I answered them all and tried to make sure he got a full picture of the properties available to him in a particular loft-styled building. As we finished talking, he apologized for taking me away from my vacation, and I told him, "This is how we do business. We take care of people. We're here for you anytime to answer questions, and we believe in being ultra-responsive."

When I returned to Atlanta, I met Ralph at a loft condominium community and showed him a unit of particular interest. I also brought information about other units on the market and sales data for those that had recently closed. I wanted to be fully armed if he wanted to write an offer on one. Ralph was one of the most curious guys I'd met in some time, asking a myriad of questions about the market, the community, my team, and how I ran my business. But I just chalked it up as his being very inquisitive. As I was showing him the last available property in the building, he said, "Rick, I have to come clean. I work for Fannie Mae." He paused to let his confession sink in, and then he asked, "Do you know who we are?"

To be honest, I really wasn't completely sure how I fit into his puzzle, but I was all ears! At that point, foreclosures in our market weren't very common. I'll never forget his next words to me, "Listen, we need a broker like you who is on the ball, runs his sales business like a company, and employs people like Paula. Would it be okay if we send you ten homes per month—or possibly more—to sell on behalf of Fannie Mae?"

That's how I got into the foreclosure business. Again, the *who* (Paula's expertise and my availability) paved the way for the *what* (a new world of handling foreclosures) in my business.

I could have never predicted that "Ralph" would be a pivotal client. However, I was ready because I kept my eyes and ears open. I poured myself into each client, but I gave more attention when I thought it could be a critical situation or person of high influence and capacity. I refused to allow myself to "water the weeds." That's a term I use when people invest time and energy into a person or situation that's unlikely to produce a good outcome. Some situations and people simply don't add value, so investing in them is a drain on time and energy. When a relationship becomes a distraction from my journey, I quit investing at a significant level. That's not hardhearted. It's actually the choice Jesus made when people weren't responsive to him.

I learned early on that who you're in business with really matters. To this day, Ralph would likely tell you I'm a good guy, that he appreciated the relationship we built, and that he respected the performance of our team as we've represented Fannie Mae over the years, selling a few thousand homes. (For perspective, typical successful realtors sell twelve to twenty-four homes a year, and we sold over 500 in 2010 and 2011, thanks in part to Ralph giving our team a shot.) But when all is said and done, he'd also tell you that the moment he knew we'd be great partners was the first impression Paula made on him on his first call to my office while I was on vacation. That turned out to be the deal-maker. First impressions are king, and the person who takes that first call is instrumental to any business. Simply returning calls in a timely manner and with sincere enthusiasm will put you ahead of eighty percent of your competition.

In addition to working consistently toward developing the right people, you must also find the best avenues for developing those relationships. I learned early in my career that handwritten notes are one of the best ways to stand out and make a relational impact in this age of emails. I consider hand-writing letters a wise use of my time. In fact, I've instructed my assistant to place five letters on my desk each day to keep me in the habit. Gratitude and thoughtful acknowledgments are gifts we all crave. An email is gone in a second and often deleted before being seen, but a handwritten note is never missed and often kept on a desk or countertop well after reading because it speaks genuine appreciation to the person who receives it. No matter what's written, the underlying message to my team member is: "You made it clear, that person matters, and you left a strong impression. You took time to do what most people won't. You're a star!"

The path to success begins with a consistent work ethic. However, if you're not careful, your work ethic can work against you. You must do things that logically take you where you want to go. Don't let yourself get sidetracked. Just keep the main thing the main thing, and the main thing is *people*.

Unwillingness to Delegate (Your Worth Per Hour)

Working hard doesn't mean doing *everything*. Gary Keller always says, "There is no task too small to delegate or outsource." During my first year as a real estate agent, my mentor walked into my office and audibly gasped. He looked at the papers covering my desk, files everywhere, and me in the middle of the sea of madness. I was fighting with my computer, frazzled and overwhelmed. He asked, "What are you *doing*?"

I said, "I'm trying to figure out how to use Mail Merge in Microsoft Word so I can send out these mailers."

I'll never forget his response: "WHY?"

Frustrated and not in the mood for a lesson, I told him that I needed to get my name out more in a specific neighborhood. I was going to try some mass mailings.

He didn't accept my lame excuse. "No, *why* are you doing this? You are clearly terrible with paper. Hire someone who is good with paper."

I looked around my office and finally saw what he saw. He was right. I didn't have a knack with paper, computers, or anything in between. Within a week, I had hired Paula, who was an absolute godsend. She had finished law school and then discovered she didn't want to be a lawyer. She was sharp and good with everything relating to paper and computers.

I paid her $8 per hour plus a small bonus for closed transactions, and she did a fantastic job for me while she was figuring out what she wanted to do with her life. More importantly, I quit doing $8-per-hour work. This experience was in 1996 when $8 an hour was top dollar! But even if you outsource $15 to $20 an hour in today's economy, top salespeople make well in excess of $100 an hour when creating and closing transactions.

One sure way to derail your wealth-building goals is to try to do everything yourself. My mentor often said, "Paper doesn't pay you a nickel. People pay you." It was a reminder that I had to spend my time meeting with people, improving my people skills, and building a network of great people. I had to force myself to stop doing most everything else.

Do you know what you're worth, per hour? I ask this question in many of my workshops. The agents tend to guess $50 to $125 per hour. Then I have them do the math. They see that that they are working fifty to sixty hours per week, but not getting the actual results they want regarding income, which translates to about $10 to $20 per hour or less! That revelation tends to get their attention. If you receive a salary, this is easy to calculate: divide the hours you work into the money you bring home. If commissioned sales or salary and commission is your compensation structure, the same process will lead you to the "per hour value" of your work.

When you perform the math above and find that your dollar per hour is lower than expected, especially in an environment with bonuses attached to performance or commission based income, it's likely because you are still doing all the paperwork, updating their websites, creating and sending marketing or collateral out weekly, sending their own newsletters, answering every incoming call. They still do minimum-wage work and it's bringing their salary down. To build wealth, you must build your business, not simply work your job. The 80/20 rule always applies. Simply put, 20% of your time typically produces 80% of the bottom-line results. The other 80% has to get done, but possibly not by you—it can be outsourced or sub-contracted, which then allows you to spend more time with highest most impactful income activities! (Note: read the book, *The One Thing* by Gary Keller to gain greater clarity on how to prioritize for optimal success in work and life.)

Early in my career, I told Paula, my first admin assistant, that part of her job was to ask me every single day, "Who is your newest client today?" That kept me focused on doing the work that generated income, doing the highest value work possible. That was an important part of my 20%, and I did it 100% of the time. Her job description was to manage all the other tasks associated with the process of marketing, listing, selling and closing real estate deals. Delegating to her changed my productivity, income production, and ultimately, my career and life trajectory.

The papers on your desk don't make purchasing decisions. Paper doesn't connect you with investment opportunities. Paper cannot catapult you into a new level of wealth. People do that. Spend time with people and outsource the other stuff. When managed properly, talented team members and staff won't cost you money, but instead, they'll make you money. They use their expertise in what they do well (that you don't enjoy doing), and you can operate free of distractions to focus on what the organization needs most (that you were made to do). Even in a corporate environment, ask yourself how much of your time is wasted in the weeds of process and paper (the 80%) instead of focusing on the 20% of rich initiatives that move the needle in your role and for your company? Entrepreneurs (and employees with an entrepreneurial attitude) earn significantly more than those who "just do their jobs." The value added to the organization is obvious. If your current environment doesn't reward high energy, focus on collaboration, respect fresh ideas and use leverage for greater results—whatever it takes, make a change.

I've consulted many salespeople and small business owners over the years, and I've discovered that many hard-charging drivers that are taking on the world alone share a misconception that they can "do things better or more efficiently" than other people, so they don't give tasks away. I hear it often: "It's faster to do it myself," and "No one can do it like I can." The real issue is that they're afraid of hiring due to their inexperience, a bad experience in the past with a poor choice in a candidate, or fear that the additional overhead will eat into their income flow. However, if you follow a good hiring plan, utilize assessment tools, and ask the right questions (natural style, skills, past successes and failures, and goals now and in five years), a truly bad hire is almost impossible to make. Even if it's not a perfect hire, the experience will help in your next effort to attract the perfect candidate.

Additionally, if you hire someone, you'll need to train them and set up accountability standards. That takes some time and effort, of course, but when you regain ten to forty hours a week of your time and invest it in your $100+ per hour activities, you'll be blown away by the impact of a quality hire. The presence of team members also creates an inherent level of accountability in your approach to work because someone is watching over you every day! Create a rich, affirming corporate culture so team members are connected to the mission of your company. When these people show up each day and you're operating with integrity, your attention to performance and productivity will skyrocket.

Leverage doesn't always mean hiring a full-time employee either. It's perfectly fine to outsource or sub-contract some types of support and not make direct hires if you don't need fulltime help. Whether it's administration, telemarketing, or marketing, or as simple as a runner or personal assistant to help with commitments at home (aka chores!), many individuals seeking flexibility and companies that specialize in your specific area of need can help you on a project or hourly basis. (In today's world, using international support staff is becoming more common. One example of a company specializing in relatively inexpensive, remote clerical and marketing support (virtual assistants) is My Out Desk. You can find them at www.myoutdesk.com.)

Let me challenge your thinking: If you hire real talent for a support role and focus more time on your higher dollar productive activities, I guarantee you'll *never* want to take back an assignment or a piece of their role. If you care about your service or product and the impact on your clients, you'll love having them on the team because they'll make you look good every day. Get past your ego and fear. I fully understand the life of an "A-type" who wants to impact everything personally. ("Save, solve, and cure" was my mantra, and I pursued it at any cost on behalf of a client.) But I've learned over the years that no one cares that *you* did it; they just care that it was done and done well. As I got busier, I started dropping balls and was often late to return calls, slow to execute marketing, and failing to meet administrative mandates while chasing the "big rocks." When I intentionally started focusing only on *the* big rock, everything changed for the better. Not only was delegation my gift and superpower, but I gave someone else the opportunity to use their superpowers alongside me.

But what about jobs where your work is part of someone else's 80%? My opinion is that everyone and every task has an 80/20 ratio, so 20% of your role is most vital. I'd suggest you take a hard look to identify what you do that has the biggest impact on the bottom line, helps those on your team generate leads for new business or monitors the financial metrics of high-level profit—all of these be tweaked or improved. Focus most of your time there. And if there's a way to invest more time in your 20%, delegate to a less expensive resource for the 80%. You'll bring more value to the organization, enhance opportunities and make a greater impact.

Get out of your own way and delegate anything not in your twenty percent and highest ROI per hour!

Examine your typical week for any signs of unbelief creeping in, inconsistent work ethic, or a reluctance to delegate. Any of those pitfalls will slow you down, if not stop you in your tracks. Deal with the problem. Reset your belief-o-meter if you need to. And get back to wealth building and the most productive use of your time!

YOU CAN DO IT!

Wealth building is all about generating cash flow and income beyond your needs, based on a workable budget, then parlaying excess capital into investments so they work for you instead of you working for every dollar needed to fund a perfect life. Remember, the most powerful investments are the ones that take little time and effort, with minimal stress to execute and maintain. They are the ones that earn income while you sleep and whether you go to work or not. That's real wealth. This strategy creates a dream life and a legacy to be proud of. The tips in this chapter are designed to inspire you to rethink your mindset, goals, spending habits and budget, as well as shift your income-producing perspective to alter your financial future.

I believe in transparency—we only win when we share our best ideas, support each other and grow together. In that light, I've shared my story about wealth building. I would be mortified to think anyone perceived my honesty as boasting. I assure you, it was slow going early on, but I kept swinging. One day, I looked at my personal financial statement and was shocked! It was far bigger and better than I'd ever imagined. I've had many successes (and plenty of failures too), but I kept chopping wood on the right side of Kyosaki's grid, regularly adding assets. Today, I have to pinch myself that I get to be me. I wasn't born with any wealth at all. I developed a perspective and skills through education, observing people, trial, error and consistent, sincere effort—complete with blood, sweat and tears. I *gave* my best to *become* my best, and it paid off. It didn't happen suddenly. It was more like watching water simmer for days, weeks and even years before coming to a boil. When the markets crashed and personal circumstances went south, I suffered setbacks and had to regroup. Building wealth is far more like cooking in a crock pot than a microwave. The microwave mindset, "I want it NOW!" rarely wins the wealth-building game.

QUESTIONS TO CONSIDER:

1. What is your definition of wealth? Is your current mindset supportive of your goals?

   Does your current plan support a trajectory that is inspiring? Is your income, budget, savings and investment plan clearly detailed and in writing?

   Are you satisfied inspired by your current job, Job performance, and belief it will serve in your growth and income goals? If not, what risks do you need to take to ensure it does?

2. How are you set with each of the "big four" necessities: cash, credit, expertise, and influence?

3. How would your friends, family members, and coworkers describe your work ethic?

4. In what ways are you "watering the weeds"? What changes could you make to maximize the use of your time, talent, and resources? Who do you need to spend more time with and in some cases less time with that don't serve with your mission, vision and values?

5. How have you encountered each of the pitfalls on the way to financial success?

- Unbelief

- Inconsistent work ethic

- Unwillingness to delegate

6. Who do you need in your life and your organization who will elevate your success through positive partnership, strategic delegation and direct impact on the work product you deliver?

CHAPTER 11

SUCCESS HACKS

If you've read all the way through this book and arrived here, at the final chapter, I want to congratulate you. Too many people today are prone to start a new project or worthwhile pursuit with good intentions and great ambition, but lose interest when another big idea grabs their fancy. They've set all kinds of potentially valuable goals, but haven't stuck to any of them. If you're still reading, that bodes well for your business future. Perseverance will serve you well in the business world.

Of course, I suspect that other people may have liked the book's title, skimmed through the Table of Contents, and skipped directly to this chapter. Why go through a proven and methodical process requiring much thought and attention if you can learn all the shortcuts instead?

Let's be clear about what I mean by success hacking. It's simply building on the experience of others and putting what they've already learned into action. The key to winning sooner and with less stress is to fast-track proven models. It makes no sense to start every business endeavor from scratch, determined to discover and do everything completely on your own. As they say, there's no need to reinvent the wheel.

Personally, I think success hacking is an appealing concept that makes perfect sense. However, it's just a first step—a bit of a head-start to get you going. You also must bring your own contributions to the table. Success hacking does *not* mean discounting your experience, judgment, and gut instincts. Just because an idea works for someone else doesn't automatically mean it will work best for you—or even at all. You still must do the work to discover and implement the ideas and systems that accommodate your specific needs.

It only makes sense to try to learn from our predecessors' discoveries . . . and mistakes. I sometimes think about the earliest humans before any level of civilization had developed. Am I the only one who wonders how they decided what to eat, and what *not* to eat? How many of them gave their lives so that the eight billion of us currently on earth now know, "That's not a good food source. That stuff'll kill you!" And those ancient cave paintings we keep discovering: were they some of the first hacks to let future tribes know, "These are the scary animals you need to run away from" or "This is how you hold your spear if you want to bring down a mastodon"?

Isaac Newton was one of the greatest minds who ever lived, yet he wrote, "If I have seen further it is by standing on the shoulders of Giants."[25] He used success hacks, and look where it got him! So if someone else's roadmap can get you a little farther along on your quest to fulfill your goals, I see nothing wrong with that.

Just keep in mind the sound advice of the old saying, "Don't believe everything you hear and only half of what you read." One size does not fit all, especially in pursuit of a life well lived and in discovering what is most fulfilling for you. This is your life; you're both the director and lead actor in it. Clarifying what you *don't* want is just as important as knowing what you do want. With that in mind, let's look at a few success hacks for you to consider.

STAY POSITIVE!

For anyone aiming for a bigger life, job one is mental toughness. This includes a positive attitude, but it's more than that—it's wearing a Teflon suit each day to defend against negative events, negative experiences and especially, negative people. When I stay in a positive mental and emotional space, my thoughts remain grounded and my body is less stressed. Stress is a huge problem for most achievers, but it can be controlled. Hal Elrod or Gary Keller's energy plan I shared earlier in Chapter 8 helps immensely. I'm sure you're like me: you work really hard to please people and make a difference every day, but even with the best of intentions, we often come up short and let people down. And when we fail to meet our goals, we feel we've let ourselves down. We know we could've done better, but we shouldn't get down on ourselves. If we're striving to become better and pushing ourselves to grow, it's not *if*, but *when* disappointment will occur. Let me share three steps that help me stay positive:

Step 1: If you've tried your best but things haven't worked out, let it go. Imagine yourself as a superhero wearing an impenetrable Kevlar suit. When you realize, "I can't control it," let the blow bounce off you and move on. Dwelling on the "what ifs" and "if onlys" will weigh you down and kill your spirit for a season . . . and maybe longer.

Step 2: If you can fix a bad situation, do it! Always do your very best to fix issues as soon as possible—especially with a relationship that matters. If that's not possible, go back to Step 1.

Step 3: Love yourself anyway. Give yourself the benefit of the doubt. Keep learning and growing with each experience. The higher-powered version of you lies on the other side of failure. Progress will lead to the best you, so learn to see failure as a classroom, not a prison. Life happens *for* you, not *to* you.

DEVELOP YOUR COMMUNICATION SKILLS

I appreciate the teaching of Miguel Ruiz. His book, *The Four Agreements*, transformed my life in one sitting. He articulates four agreements that continue to eliminate a lot of unnecessary stress for me and have enhanced countless relationships, both personally and professionally. To summarize the four:

1. *Be impeccable with your word.* Be precise, thoughtful and considerate in how you communicate. Words—and the energy behind them—are a powerful force. Work on your communication skills every day.

2. *Don't take anything personally.* When people act in anger, self-pity, smothering with attention or demands, or any other kind of manipulation, that's on them, not you. Taking their actions and words personally is like accepting their cancer and allowing yourself to suffer unnecessarily.

3. *Don't make assumptions.* I've fallen prey to this countless times, and more often than not, my assumption about another person's motive was inaccurate. Stay curious and ask lots of good questions. When you quickly make assumptions, you become either offensive or defensive, and then it's really hard to find common ground. If something bothers you, ask for clarification; don't assume the worst.

4. *Always do your best.* In all situations, do your best and be okay with it. That's all you can do. Own your shortcomings, but don't let them discourage you—and certainly, don't punish yourself for something you said or did. If you can fix it, fix it, but if not, let it go.[26]

It's very hard to raise a person's IQ, but it's possible for all of us to raise our EQ, our ability to connect effectively with others. My favorite motivational author and speaker Zig Ziglar recommends that we work on becoming more likable, which naturally leads to trust. Without trust, no one opens up and no one will lean in and support you ... or be open to your support. He said, "You can have everything in life you want, if you will just help other people get what they want." Zig had it figured out long ago! The law of reciprocity is evident in all of our relationships: Angry people get angry in return, kind people get kindness, patient people get patience, and so on. But we have the power to change a bad attitude into a good one. For instance, if you're having a bad day, write five sincere thank you notes and call a couple of people to encourage them. Don't ask for anything, don't tell them you're feeling down, and don't check up on anything they're doing. Just encourage ... and watch what that will do for your mood and energy level. You'll get a double dose of love and gratitude right back, guaranteed. Zig also asked this question: "How do you know when someone needs encouragement?" The answer is: "They're breathing!" Kindness is currency and always a good investment—not only because the law of reciprocity will repay you, but because the best version of yourself would always be kind.

We often talk about the magic of compound interest and investing for a ROI with our money and resources, but I want to challenge you to consider the power of compound kindness. That's when you take a disproportionate interest in someone else without expectations. They'll sense your sincere and selfless intentions, and you'll compound the impact. As an action point, each day make a list of people to add value to them in a meaningful way, and make it part of your strategic plan. Then watch the awesome power of compounding kindness!

LISTEN TO YOUR HEART

I'm an advocate of listening to your inner voice when uncertainty creeps into a situation or relationship. If something feels "off," stay curious and not judgmental. Give it time to see if your initial impression was right or if new information changes your perception. But if your heart says go for it, go for it. If it's a big decision or commitment, it's a good idea to seek wise counsel, but again, listen to your heart. Intuition is hardwired into your soul. Pay attention to it.

In a fascinating article in *Harvard Business Review,* Melody Wilding reports that intuition is a valuable leadership quality. She roots her observations in the science of neurology: "When you approach a decision intuitively, your brain works in tandem with your gut to quickly assess all our memories, past learnings, personal needs, and preferences and then makes the wisest decision given the context. In this way, intuition is a form of emotional and experiential data that leaders need to value." Many people, Wilding notes, confuse intuition with fear. They have difficulty sorting out negative feelings—guilt, fear, anger, and doubt—from a sixth sense of helpful perception. She explains:

> Leaders who identify as highly sensitive have stronger gut feelings than most, but have also been discouraged from using this sensory data. The trait of high sensitivity contributes to perceiving, processing, and synthesizing information more deeply, including data about others' emotional worlds. This means your intuition is more highly developed than most other people because you're constantly adding new data to your bank of knowledge about the world and yourself. The only problem is that you've probably been taught to devalue this strength in yourself.

The good news is that intuition is like a muscle—it can be strengthened with intentional practice.[27]

It's good advice to exercise those muscles, especially if you've neglected them far too long.

JOY THROUGH GENEROSITY

Another life hack is increasing joy through generosity. I really like the idea of "vibrational giving" that Andres Pira describes in his book, *Homeless to Billionaire*. It works by giving to causes when your heart is naturally drawn to them. I do my best to live by the mantra straight from Jesus' teachings that if someone asks, give. However, in practice this simple concept needs some discernment. I need to gauge the amount I give by the level of authenticity and need I sense (again, listening to my heart). I've chosen to give whether the need is time, connections or money.

In the past, I've sometimes worried that people might take advantage of me. I've overcome that fear by giving with no strings attached, and I view loans as gifts. The responsibility to use the money wisely is always on the person or organization. If I'm tricked by a panhandler or fraudster, that's on them too. In the end, I'm satisfied if I've followed my heart and I'm clear about my motives. Maintaining that perspective has saved me countless hours of unnecessary worry about outcomes I can't control. This is particularly important for my personal sanity when it comes to loaning money to friends and family!

But there's another aspect to Andre's description of vibrational giving that applies to your time and focus. If your heart says lean in, do it! Vibrational giving shows up in many ways. Don't miss the chance to help someone or you'll short the universe a gift and deny yourself the joy of making a difference, which is the greatest gift you can give yourself. Even though this goes against the 80/20 principle, I sincerely hope those who know me best will inscribe, "He never said no" on my gravestone. I love serving people, and I love saying "yes" to requests as often as possible. It's not always expensive, complicated or hard.

IN MANY CASES, YOU HAVE TO SIMPLY STOP AND LISTEN FOR OPPORTUNITIES TO SERVE. QUITE OFTEN, IT'S AS SIMPLE AS BEING A FRIEND AND GENUINELY LISTENING.

Let me share an example of vibrational giving. It happened on a foggy morning in Alpharetta, Georgia. I was on the way to the gym early on a Saturday morning. At a stop light, I caught a glimpse of a woman standing behind her car about forty yards away in the middle of an empty parking lot. She was waving frantically. I thought, *Surely, she's not waiving at me.* The previous evening I'd seen a news report about scammers who drive up behind cars and bump them to get drivers to pull over to look at the damage. They then steal the car and leave the driver on the side of the road . . . or maybe in this case, in the parking lot. The woman looked suspicious, and I wondered if this was a variation of the scam. I didn't want show up on the evening news for something like that! My mind raced for a reason to ignore the frantic waving and drive off. *What if a gunman was in the back seat or hiding nearby to pounce on me when I'm unarmed and alone?* It was so early that there were very few cars driving by—this was the definition of "secluded." I continued to stack up reasons to drive away, but after a few more negative thoughts raced through my mind, I reached into my heart for a positive answer and it screamed, *Go over and see what she needs!*

I slowly pulled into the parking lot and approached her. As I rolled my window down, I realized her hand wasn't on top of the trunk lid.

She had shut the trunk on her hand! She had her hand in the wrong place when she pressed the button to close her trunk, and her keys were in her purse in the car. And her baby was screaming in the backseat. No wonder she was frantic! I quickly opened her door and pushed the trunk release. I don't think I've ever seen a woman more relieved and grateful for such a simple act of service. Her hand was surprisingly unharmed. She pulled her child out for a loving hug, and the world seemed right again. As we stood together for a few minutes, she told me that a lot of cars had stopped at the light, but I was the only one who bothered to stop to help her. I didn't tell her that I'd thought of a dozen reasons to join that group of drivers. I'd been a little slow, but my inner voice was persistent enough to prompt me to stop to help her.

For me situations like this are multi-faceted experiences: I listen to my inner voice, assess any risk or danger, confirm the energy behind the compulsion, and then act accordingly. I try to always lean toward the generous part in me that wants to give and help and serve. It's the most powerful version of me—the one I like best, the one that feels abundant and generous in all ways. And it's in you too.

THE POWER OF SELF-IMPOSED SAVING

I included the value of "forced saving" in the previous chapter, among my list of good reasons to own real estate. Technically, the term is one coined by economists to refer to a financial situation (either unintentional or by design) that reduces consumers' disposable income so they're unable to spend as usual. I use the term too, although what I mean it is that you force *yourself* to save—your spending restrictions are self-imposed.

Why would someone want to do that? Because if you ever want to start wealth building, you must be very intentional about how to get started. If you don't change your habits, it never happens.

David Bach, in his book, *The Automatic Millionaire*, asks why people commit eight to ten hours a day, a tedious commute, and most of their energy to a job only to earn a check that goes to creditors, the government, and everyday necessities. He points out that we tend to pay everyone else first, and then if anything is left over, we pay ourselves. His advice is "pay yourself first"—completely redirect your income so you receive something from every check.[28]

I agree with Bach about paying yourself first, but I know from experience that it's too difficult to do without help. It's critical to set up a system that *forces* you to win rather than one that relies on your willpower, so I designed my own "System of Forced Savings."

The basic idea is that you must design a structure that *requires* you to pay yourself rather than hoping you will have something left at the end of every paycheck. I use my system in real estate, but it can be applied to other investment vehicles as well.

My algorithm for success is simple. I have an asset-minded mentality. My assets take priority over my liabilities. My investments come before my fun purchases. In other words, I will do whatever it takes to ensure that I put money into my assets (savings) before any leisure items or activities. I don't buy consumable, non-appreciating purchases with credit cards. I use cash for the fun stuff. My credit cards are paid off in full every month. The interest you pay is extremely high and adds up quickly. Minimum payments will never pay off a credit card, and many banks charge well in excess of twelve percent interest.

It is this forced savings system that was behind the investment strategy I previously recommended if you want to retire a millionaire. You simply purchase ten rental properties that rent for more than the carrying costs creating a positive net income and pay them off prior to retiring. By paying the mortgages each month, you are forcing yourself to save. Would you naturally put that kind of cash away without the real estate purchases? Probably not!

"But Rick," you might argue, "how do I know if the real estate is a good purchase?" Every real estate purchase will pay for itself if you hold it long enough and the rental market is strong enough to cover your costs (principal, interest, taxes, insurance, and maintenance). You just need the cash or earning power to carry your real estate investment through the market ups and downs. I own three commercial properties and each building carries its own weight. I have no reason to sell when each one is paying for itself every month.

If your chosen method to wealth is through real estate, you must ask yourself, "How can I force myself to pay for my real estate holdings *before* I pay for my groceries?" The key is boosting income while sticking tightly enough to your budget to still cover your core needs, but after investing each month! Working out the details may take time and require the help of several professionals, but it's worth it.

AUTOMATIC WITHDRAWALS

If real estate is not the investment for you, you can set up automatic withdrawal of funds from your paycheck or earnings to ensure you pay for your investments first. Make it inconvenient to spend money earmarked for investments. Make it impossible to fail. Mo Anderson, former CEO and cultural icon at Keller Williams, taught us the simple formula of living off seventy percent of your net income, giving or tithing ten percent, investing ten percent, and saving ten percent. Over time this commitment will serve you well, especially if you adopt the strategy early in your life. If you're a bit behind, find a way to live off fifty percent and double up on investing and saving for investments. Also master the art of budgeting to live within your means. I highly recommend Mo's book, *A Joy Filled Life*. Her story of humble beginnings that led to co-owning and running the fastest growing and now largest real estate company in the U.S. will captivate and inspire you.

Committing to a budget with an automated savings and investing strategy is working for me in many areas of wealth building and giving. For example, I established a whole life insurance policy quite a few years ago that has grown quite quickly and to a level I wouldn't have imagined when I was younger. My good friend John White at Northwestern Mutual taught me about the benefits of automatically withdrawing larger amounts of money each month for whole life insurance because it has so many benefits. Not only do I breathe easier knowing my family is taken care of should I unexpectedly pass, but I can borrow against that money without paying interest. In other words, I can stash cash in this policy, and when the market shifts, I'll have the cash ready to invest. I also use automated withdrawals to invest in the stock market. My profit-share at Keller Williams goes into a separate savings account for strategic giving. If every dollar in income goes straight to your general checking account, you'll quickly find ways to spend it, and often not in prudent ways.

I also want to leave my family a financial legacy and a charitable trust for causes that matter. Insurance and a carefully written will, perhaps including a trust, guarantee that your estate will be managed properly. Taxes are your greatest expense, and estate taxes are no different. Proper planning with tax and accounting experts is priceless, and the earlier you craft a plan, the better it works for you and your family. Why not plan now for a positive future regardless of the ultimate timing and outcome? You'll sleep better because you'll know that your hard work has lasting power—a legacy that matters!

When the market declines, those who really win are the people with ample cash, credit, and valued assets. I learned this the hard way! So, while the market is strong, I try to accumulate cash and wait for the next big shift. The market shifts approximately every eight to ten years, so I need to get ready. We are in a booming market now, so I am utilizing my system of forced savings to prepare for the next downturn.

Timing matters. It is critical to choose the right form of forced savings based on the market and the opportunities before you. Should you stash away money in your 401(k)? Should you force yourself to save through whole term life insurance? Should you purchase a rental property or a commercial property? The answer to each of those questions is, "It depends on the time."

Warren Buffet famously said, "When everyone else is buying, I am selling." He knows what he's talking about, so I don't recommend making decisions based on what everyone else is doing. Instead, find a team of skilled professionals to advise you. They will keep you from making emotional decisions about your money . . . and none of us are above those emotional decisions!

A while back, I fell in love with a local guitar store, but eventually I heard that the store was in financial trouble. I wanted to help the owner because I truly liked him, and I think his store is one of the great ones. I thought I knew the music industry, and I'm passionate about music, especially guitars. Without consulting my team, I invested. Clearly, it was an investment based on emotion rather than facts.

If I had followed my own rules and consulted my team, I would never have invested. My rules include:

1. Consult at least three trusted professional experts in that arena before investing;

2. Go three deep with references; (ask references for references; by the third one, you'll typically get a sense of the entire truth)

3. Give yourself a wait period before investing; and

4. Whenever possible, invest in arenas where you can bring expertise and influence to the table.

Mine wasn't a wise decision in terms of the return on my investment. I didn't feel too bad about it because I was backing a person and an establishment that I respected. The cash I'd saved was strategically tagged for speculative investing. Still, I can't afford to make many other such decisions and expect to build wealth. Be wise in your investments and make the most of the money you're forcing yourself to save. Sometimes you win and sometimes you learn. This was a clear example of a lesson I was meant to discover. Just because you've enjoyed success in one arena doesn't make you an automatic winner in all situations. Who you're in business with (reflected in character, experience, and expertise) is often the most critical indicator of potential success.

In a horse race, some recommend, "Bet on the jockey, not the horse." That's a good starting place because it takes both a good jockey and a good horse to win a race. One thing's for sure, if you put an inexperienced rider on a purebred racehorse, you'll never win! "Winners win" is a self-evident truth, but we should also pay attention to losses and be bold enough to ask hard questions about them. All winners have losses, and if someone says they have no losses to share, back away slowly . . . or maybe it's better to run! Your gut will serve as an internal sonar—never ignore the sense that something isn't right. If pausing feels appropriate, take more time to analyze the opportunity. If the opportunity is available "today only," it's probably not a good one. If it looks too good to be true in terms of projected returns, it probably is.

Limit yourself to investments that are backed by expertise and can provide references that confirm success. When investing with a seasoned successful expert with a track record of more wins than losses, chances go up you'll win with them too.

Wishing for more money won't work. Hoping never makes it happen. Take the time to set up a system of forced savings and then make investments you feel confident about . . . and stick to it.

KNOW . . . HAVE . . . DO

One of my Keller Williams heroes is a leader named Gene Rivers. I recently heard him tell about a moment that changed his life. He was living in Miami when hurricane Hugo blew the roof off his house. He and his wife, Rebecca, woke up after the ordeal with nothing but a mattress over their heads. Terrified of living in the path of another hurricane, they decided it was time to move. But where? They agreed to move anywhere in the United States where they thought they could be truly successful. They pulled out a map and asked themselves, "Where is the market expanding? Do we see a place where we can move and dominate the market?"

Gene and Rebecca now own The Rivers Team in Tallahassee, Florida, and have been the number one sales team in that area for years. They are hyper successful beyond personal sales as well owning multiple Keller Williams market centers and many investment properties as well. They made a plan and worked the plan relentlessly. They didn't leave their success to chance, but began to live a much more strategic life in the best location for their skillset. It took a hurricane to give them the resolve to make such a bold move.

Gene is a phenomenal sales trainer and coach and often asks his audiences, "How many of you have big, lofty goals?" Without fail, most hands are flung into the air excitedly. He then asks, "How many of you are absolutely certain you are going to reach those goals?" Slowly, the hands fall as listeners realize they don't have a plan to move forward. Bewildered, he asks them "why?" – when there are countless books, role models, coaches and classes that can lead you to road maps and blue printed success.

How about you? By now you should have identified several clear goals. But are you confident you will meet them? Do you need a strategic relaunch or move to a more fertile market area or business more suited to your skillset and passion? If you're not sure, you can think it through with three simple words: *Know*, *Have*, and *Do*. One of those words will help you solve every riddle.

First, do you *know* exactly what you are trying to accomplish and do you have the knowledge to make it happen? If not, empower yourself with the confidence you need by obtaining that specific knowledge: take a class, ask a mentor for advice, or simply watch some YouTube videos. Start down the path of knowledge until you obtain the understanding or perspective needed for your journey.

When you are certain that you know everything necessary to accomplish your goals, then ask yourself, "Do I *have* everything I need to get this job done?" Are you selling something that is truly in demand? Is your business scalable? Are you in an expanding market? If not, you may be in a place where your best option is to move to a new market. Find a new job. Change your business. And then commit like never before. A committed heart cannot be denied!

In his book, *Crush It!*, Gary Vaynerchuk challenges his readers, "Live your passion. What does that mean anyway? It means when you wake up every morning, every single morning, you are pumped because you get to talk about or work with or do the thing that interests you most in the world."[29]

I absolutely agree with Gary. If you are not in a business where you are pumped about your industry, get out. Find something you're passionate about, where you jump out of bed every morning, ready to take on the world.

But a word of caution here: don't confuse your hobby with your industry. I learned in my twenties that my passion for music should remain a hobby. I discovered that only .02 percent or less of all guitarists were talented enough to become wealthy through their music, and I knew I wasn't among that elite percentage. Playing the guitar and writing music have remained an important part of my life, but I pursued a different passion to fund my musical pursuits.

Finally, you must evaluate every day what you *do* to ensure you're on the right track and still working to achieve your goals. If you're not confident you can meet them, why have them as goals to begin with?

Annual goals serve a purpose, but are too abstract and too distant for monitoring daily progress and achievement. The war is won *daily*, not monthly and annually. Learn to subdivide your annual plan into bite-sized, daily chunks, and then create a daily plan that plots your path to your highest and best ROI on that time, effort, and energy.

I like to take my annual goals and divide them into nine months (January through September)—*not* twelve months. I've repeatedly found that if I'm behind in the fourth quarter, it's near impossible to catch up during November and December with so many holiday distractions. If I stay on track through September, I can catch my breath during the fourth quarter, guilt-free. If not, hopefully I'm close enough to my goals to dial up a strong fourth quarter and crush it anyway.

THE CONSCIOUS COMPETENCE LADDER

As I come to the end of this book, I realize I've been barraging you with a lot of information that may be new to you, and challenges that some might consider intimidating. Your emotions may be fluctuating, jumping from fear and trepidation to joyous enthusiasm, to self-doubt, to steadfast determination. If so, there's a reason for that.

In the 1970s a man named Noel Burch was an employee of Gordon Training International, now a widely recognized human relations training organization, but then still a rather young organization. While there, Burch developed a matrix that came to be known as the Conscious Competence Ladder. It has four stages[30]:

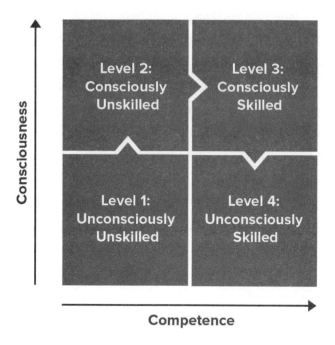

At Level 1, people don't know how much they don't know. They are "blissfully ignorant." Their confidence far exceeds their skills. This is point where the input of others and some basic assessment tests, along with a lot of positive feedback, are extremely helpful for identifying strengths and weaknesses. Eventually, they are ready to move on to the next stage.

Level 2 is when they realize they need specific skills. They discover what they need to know, but are unnerved to admit they don't know how to do it. Such a realization has a demoralizing effect on some people, and they will need help with staying positive. Improving self-confidence takes time, but it is necessary for long-term growth and accomplishing bold goals. The good news is that we can learn things we don't know, and when we do, we move on up the ladder.

At Level 3, people become more positive and self-assured. Their abilities to do the job have caught up with their awareness of what needs to be done. It's a good feeling and a confidence builder. As they keep at it, this is the "practice makes perfect" stage.

The rise to Level 4 is almost imperceptible. High performance requires less conscious effort; it's almost automatic. Of course, if you stop using this new skill for a while, you can drop back down the ladder to Level 3. (One way to prevent this is to teach the skill to others.) And if you want to keep growing after you get to Level 4 with one skill, you can start over with other new skills.

Michael Jordan is an example of this progression. As a kid in Wilmington, North Carolina, he didn't know what he didn't know about basketball. He simply wanted to enjoy the game (Level 1: unconscious incompetence). He tried out for the team when he was a sophomore in high school, but he was cut and sent to the junior varsity to "further develop" the skills required to compete at the high school level. The story goes that he locked himself in his room and cried his eyes out. At that moment, he became consciously aware of his incompetence (Level 2: conscious incompetence). It didn't help that his best friend, Leroy Smith, made it on the varsity squad. Leroy was 6-foot-7, Michael was 5-foot-10.

But through practice and determination, Michael improved. He didn't give up on his ability to shoot and play the game, and he grew four inches that season. He made the most of his time on the JV squad. Thanks to physical growth, coupled with hard work and good coaching, he went on to have a successful high school career. At Level 3, he was a star for the North Carolina Tar Heels. By the time he graduated and was drafted by the Chicago Bulls, he was at Level 4. Jordan became one of the most storied and successful basketball players of all time. When he was young, every shot he took required some level of focused attention to form and technique, but over time, he was "in the zone," seemingly weightless as he floated high above the rim and impervious to the competitors attempting to stop him. But he didn't do it alone. It also took a talented team and a supporting cast of coaches and trainers.

In one way, we're all "like Mike": in every new goal and endeavor, we start hopeful and uncertain in the Level 1 position. Most people quit just before the magic happens. Then, we realize what we don't know and can't do well. "Conscious incompetence" is an awkward time, but it offers maximum opportunity to grow and improve. If you're committed, you know you have to level up, grind, and learn like never before. The goal matters, and failure isn't an option. Constant practice makes all the difference. We could draft an equation: "Time on task over time = expertise," or another way of putting it is: "Plenty of experience produces expertise." As you practice, you'll improve until you reach a place where it comes naturally, without conscious thought of how you do it.

This progression shows the value of "failing forward." That's how we learn; that's how we grow; that's how we become experts. Success hacks don't prevent us from making mistakes, but they can teach us how to learn from them so we don't repeat them and are able to move forward faster.

I wanted to end with this Conscious Competence Ladder because it helps to explain why, as you throw yourself into your efforts to lead your best possible life, you're certain to go through all kinds of emotions. Sometimes you'll feel tentative and uncertain, and other times like everything is hunky-dory. Don't be too concerned about your mental health as your emotions swing back and forth; it happens to us all. It's highly unlikely you'll enjoy great success without bruises and pain . . . and maybe tears as well. The saying, "No pain, no gain" is popular because it's true. When I forget to open my GPS app on a trip and hit slow traffic, two things happen: I get a little upset with myself for assuming things would go smoothly, and I promise myself to use it the next time. The pain teaches me a lesson—or more accurately, it reminds me of a lesson I'd learned but ignored!

Follow your head and heart, honoring the input from mentors, economic models and proven strategies that work with predictable regularity. Align your strengths with your work as often as possible, then leverage systems, tools and people to offset your weaknesses. When you're hitting a wall, rethink and realign. Consider what and who might make a difference in the success story you're crafting. Find great role models and accountability partners for work and life so you'll continue to fine tune your approach. And make a daily decision to put in the work. Use both versions of the 1-3-5 (Crush It and Inhibitor) to confirm and reaffirm a plan to overcome limiting beliefs and conquer your goals. The last step is hardcore commitment. Go all in, 100%, and in a non-negotiable, no-way-out determination. Be crystal clear about *what* you want, *how* you'll do it, *why* you want it and *who* will help you get there.

CLOSING THOUGHTS

By virtue of the fact that you've completed this book, you've distinguished yourself from most other Americans. It is estimated that more than eighty percent of the population didn't read a single book last year, so you're automatically in the top twenty percent. In addition, you've chosen to invest your time in a book designed to help you improve your life, which puts you into an even more prestigious percentage. I hope that's reason enough for you to celebrate.

But I also hope you're now ready to put this book down and get busy applying what you've read to your business, nonprofit, organization, or personal life. You're at the end of the book, but if I didn't inspire you to take some giant steps forward on your journey to a more fulfilled, less regretful future self, I didn't accomplish what I set out to do.

Just this week, as I was finishing this chapter, I heard someone on a television interview state, "People say you only live once. I don't agree. You only *die* once; you live every day." I can't think of a better succinct summation of what I've been trying to communicate in these chapters. You only get the most out of your life if you get the most out of *each day*. Pull out your Life Wheel regularly (at least every quarter) to confirm your status in each category and make real-time, critical adjustments to stay the course you've scripted, one that leads to your best you.

It has taken years, a variety of experiences and plenty of honest feedback for me to approach my full potential, and it has been well worth it. My successes aren't primarily about money . . . and sometimes not about money at all. When I can be free from self-doubt and self-inflicted stress, I can "be in the moment" to give and receive information, support, and encouragement. It's the people who have joined me on this journey that really excite me. They've helped me grow, and I hope to some degree, I've helped them take steps to reach their best selves. Together, we work really hard and often crush our goals, and we also care a lot for each other. Profit is vital to sustainability, but I've always done my best to never put profit over people. You can have profit *and* incredibly rich relationships at work. Creating and maintaining affirming, positive relationships should be a point of great pride as you move toward your best life, one truly worth living (and even writing a book about it one day).

As I type this section of the book, I remember a dear friend who was tragically taken from us too early at only 50 years old. Rodney Camren was about as nutty as they come—hyper-social, typically too loud for a room and often inappropriate for the sake of a cheap laugh or joke.

But he was also hard working, deeply caring and thoughtful. Above all else, he was committed to self-mastery and building a business through people. His childhood was a disaster, even filing for emancipation from his neglectful parents when he was only fourteen, but he had the courage to use his heartache as a stepping stone to better things. To say he was bold is an understatement—he embodied Nietzsche's dictum, "What doesn't kill you makes you stronger." His suffering certainly made him stronger. Above all I appreciated Rodney's commitment to growth and his positive impact on every person he came into contact with. One day when I was teaching a class in my office, Rodney was cutting up and asking question after question. I could tell he was doing all that just to get under my skin—not in a bad way, but like good friends do sometimes. After the 765th question, I stopped and told him, "Rodney, one more interjection and I'm gonna slap you!"

He smiled and quickly replied, "Is that a threat or a promise? I kind of like that idea."

The other people in the room were temporarily shocked, but when they saw both of us laughing, they got the point. It was a classic Rodney moment.

Like all of us, Rodney was a work in progress. In his pursuit of progress over perfection, he never lost sight of the truth that building quality relationships is at the center of the target, our best and highest goal, the thing that makes life worth living. His ultimate gift was his kindness. He regularly offered to coach younger realtors and was always ready to help lead important initiatives in our office and the community. I thought I knew Rodney very well, but I learned some secrets about him at his funeral.

Michelle and Pam were Rodney's close friends, and they agreed to officiate his funeral. Rodney wasn't very religious, and his family had been completely missing from his life for decades, so they played no role in the service. I was asked to speak and shared thoughts about him, his life and his impact on me and others in our organization. Frankly, I knew it was going to be the hardest thing I'd ever done in front of a group.

The room at a local church was massive, but it was standing room only. There may have been a thousand people in attendance from all walks of life, far more than a typical funeral service. Michelle shared about Rodney's life, then Pam, and then me. I sat down, and someone sang a song. I thought the service was over, but it wasn't. We had only taken twenty minutes, so Pam stood up and asked if anyone wanted to say something about Rodney's impact on them. For the next hour and half, people told stories of how Rodney was always there for them. He was a trusted resource to help in countless ways, and they felt his genuine love. Many said he made them feel important. He was the first call late at night when a neighbor's cat got out and couldn't be found. He was there the moment a friend needed money or helping hand, and he was there to make the new person in a meeting feel welcomed.

By the end, I knew Rodney even better than I had before he died. He was, as they say in my part of the country, "a piece of work," but he had an enormous heart for people. He knew the true meaning of life, and he lived it out every day in every relationship. It's the little things: acts of generosity, a smile, a friendly joke, a tender hand and a ready heart to invest time and energy in people. He encouraged people wherever he went, and his kindness mended many a broken heart. He often wrote notes to people to express his love and appreciation.

I want to be more like Rodney, and I'm sure you do too. When you face your last day, I would be surprised if you're clutching your financial statements or you're concerned about an upcoming quarterly report. No, if you build an intentional life, with time and margin to lean into the relationships that matter, on that day your heart will overflow with love and thankfulness for the people you've touched and who have touched you. On the morning Rodney didn't wake up, it was too late for him to craft his eulogy, but he didn't need to write a word. He had already written it in glowing prose through his assertive, life-changing love for people.

What eulogy have you written for yourself so far? Are you thrilled with it, or does it need an editor . . . or to be completely rewritten? Every moment of every day, you're writing on the hearts of those around you. At the close of this book, take some time to write what you hope people will say at your funeral when you've drawn your last breath. Think about the people who mean the most to you, the people you rub shoulders with every day, and the seemingly chance encounters with people you pass by. It's not too late. In fact, now is the perfect time.

Do your Life Wheel, your vision, your mission and your plan reflect the heart of your eulogy, or do you need to make some changes? We've talked about alignment a lot in this book, and the alignment of your plans and your eulogy are most important. Your Five-Year-Future Self poster is the catalyst for today and beyond! If you honor all twelve categories, create an action plan and consistently move, you'll become the person you want to be, and your eulogy will write itself over time. It's never too late . . . until it is. Today is your day, and right now is your moment.

Bottom line is this: Don't settle for less than the best you can be for yourself and those you love. Your unyielding determination to plan everyday results in your ability to live a life with no regrets. That is my desire for you! When you're ready to leave your working life behind you, I don't want you to have any coulda/shoulda/woulda disappointments. Regret is a horrible thing. Do the work, and be glad you did it. A huge, purposeful life is available to you one day at a time . . . starting today.

QUESTIONS TO CONSIDER:

1. Who are some "giants" whose lives have inspired you? How have their lives influenced yours?

2. Do you currently have a system of self-imposed savings working for you? If not, do you have some other plan for wealth building?

3. Are you 100 percent confident that you'll meet your most important goal(s)? If not:

   - What do you need to *know* to reach it?

   - What resource(s) do you need to *have*?

   - What do you need to *do* (today, tomorrow, and next week) to move forward?

   - *Who* can you consult for support, role modeling, and leverage to give you a competitive advantage to ultimately attain your goals?

4. Thinking back to how you've developed skills in the past, do the steps on the Conscious Competence Ladder sound familiar? Are you currently at one of those stages while trying to acquire a new skill for a specific job?

5. Take some time to reflect and write the eulogy you hope will be spoken at your funeral or memorial service.

6. Look back at your Five-Year-Future Self and examine any goals that are out of alignment with your eulogy.

7. What is something you've learned from this book that you'll be most likely to remember?

ENDNOTES

1   Steven Pressfield, *Turning Pro: Tap Your Inner Power and Create Your Life's Work* (New York: Black Irish Entertainment, 2012), p. 20.

2   Laurie Beth Jones, *The Path* (New York: Hachette Books, 1996), pp. 71-72.

3   Many organizations encourage people to use SMART goals, including Indeed.com, https://www.indeed.com/career-advice/career-development/smart-goals

4   Simon Sinek, "Start with Why," Leadership, TED Talks.

5   Shawn Achor, *The Happiness Advantage: How a Positive Brain Fuels Success in Work and Life* (New York: Currency Books, 2010), pp. 3-4.

6   "Giving Thanks Can Make You Happier," Harvard Health Publishing, Aug. 14, 2021 https://www.health.harvard.edu/healthbeat/giving-thanks-can-make-you-happier

7   Susan David and Christina Congleton, "Emotional Agility," Harvard Business Review, Nov. 2013, https://hbr.org/2013/11/emotional-agility

8   Lolly Daskal, "13 Powerful Steps That Will Eliminate Your Self-Doubt," Inc., May 13, 2016, https://www.inc.com/lolly-daskal/13-powerful-steps-that-will-eliminate-your-self-doubt.html

9   Dr. Henry Cloud and Dr. John Townsend, *Boundaries* (Grand Rapids: Zondervan, 1992, 2017), p. 32.

10   Kevin Kruse, "The 80/20 Rule and How It Can Change Your Life," Forbes, March 7, 2016, https://www.forbes.com/sites/kevinkruse/2016/03/07/80-20-rule/?sh=4cc373803814

11   Brian Tracy, *Eat that Frog! 21 Great Ways to Stop Procrastinating and Get More Done in Less Time* (San Francisco: Berrett-Koehler Publishers, 2002), p. 9.

12   Gary Keller with Jay Papasan, *The One Thing* (London: John Murray Press, 2001).

13   Stephen R. Covey, *The 8th Habit: From Effectiveness to Greatness* (New York: Free Press, 2004), pp. 242-243.

14   Isaiah 55:9

15   https://www.cdc.gov/sleep/index.html#:~:text=Not%20getting%20 enough%20sleep%20is,injury%20and%20disability%20each%20year

16   Brian Tracy, *Eat that Frog* (Hodder Paperback, 2013), pp. 3, 52.

17   Hal Elrod, *The Miracle Morning* (Hal Elrod International, Inc., 2012).

18   Aubrey Marcus, *Own the Day, Own Your Life* (New York: Harper Wave, 2018), p. 4.

19   Shaun Rawls, *"F"-It-Less* (Forefront Books, 2021).

20   Michael J. Maher, *The 7 L's of Communication* (Dallas: BenBella, 2014), p. 164.

21   Brandon Gaille, "23 Lottery Winners Bankrupt Statistics," May 26, 2017, https://brandongaille.com/22-lottery-winners-bankrupt-statistics/

22   "$68 Trillion Assets in Motion," Cerulli Associates, https://info. cerulli.com/HNW-Transfer-of-Wealth-Cerulli.html

23   "150 Bucket List Ideas + Printables to Help You Live Your Best Life," Bestow.com, January 10, 2020, https://www.bestow.com/blog/ bucket-list-ideas/

24   Gary S. Reid and Gary M. Krebs, *Wealth Made Easy* (Dallas: BenBella, 2019), Wealth Hack #25.

25   *Bartlett's Familiar Quotations,* 17th Edition (Boston: Little, Brown and Company), p. 290.

26   Miguel Ruiz, *The Four Agreements* (San Rafael, CA: Amber-Allen Publishing, 2012).

27   Melody Wilding, "How to Stop Overthinking and Start Trusting Your Gut," Harvard Business Review, March 10, 2022, https://hbr. org/2022/03/how-to-stop-overthinking-and-start-trusting-your-gut

28   David Bach, *The Automatic Millionaire* (New York: Broadway Books, 2004).

29   Gary Vaynerchuk, *Crush It!* (New York: Harper Studio, 2009), p. 3.

30   Chart and explanation from https://www.mindtools.com/pages/ article/newISS_96.htm. Chart reproduced with permission from Gordon Training International.

ACKNOWLEDGMENTS

First, I'd like to credit God with my very existence, and although I'm not an advanced Christian in many ways, I believe it's all about the journey while living in an imperfect world and simply doing your very best. I know that God has a hand in everything that I have become, and more importantly, who I have yet to become. I've felt the gift of his spiritual protection and energy in my heart and mind since I can remember.

I'd like to thank all of those who played roles as parents in my life. All of you have made a massive difference at critical moments when I needed you the most.

My biological parents, Hubert and Gene: You are so loving, smart, and motivated . . . with self-made success stories.

My adopted father and mother, Glen and Peggy: Thank you for being there when it mattered most with consistent love and for exposing me to God.

Nancy Jo, you're amazing: I love that you adopted me into your heart as your own. That means everything to me.

Jeff, my mentor: Your timely investment in me as a young teen taught me life skills, the value and purpose of money, unlimited thinking, and a world perspective like I'd never seen before.

My sisters and brothers, sometimes from another parent and sometimes in marriage, but always dear to me: Eric, Summer and Brian, Julie and Dominic, Brandon, Joy and Boyd, Napoleon and Karina, thank you for always being there for me. I love you all!

My amazing sons, Alex, Luke, Cory and Tyler: I'm sure I'm the luckiest father in the world. I have tremendous pride in who you have become as productive and successful citizens, and most importantly, as wonderfully loving human beings. Thanks for the practice run so that one day I'll be an even better grandfather!

My inner circle of lifelong friends in my personal life and at work: You add value to every conversation and make life better each time we're together. I'd attempt to list you all by name, but I'm terrified I'd leave someone off. (Actually, the list is at least five pages long and my editor tells me that's far too long.) If you're not sure if you'd have made the list, call me and I'll happily confirm that you would have. I've been blessed with the most amazing KW family of mentors and friends, my Gobundance tribe, and also those from my music circles that evolved into bands that I've played and written music with over the years. I love and appreciate all of you!

Saving the best for last, my wife and best friend, Pauline: You have shown me loyalty and love like no other. You've taught me the value of second chances and that love is vulnerable, transparent, passionate, and sometimes fiercely honest in times of challenge and adversity. We share a great love of family, adventure, travel, live music, scuba diving, wake surfing, and so much more. You are literally the rock in my roll! I'm grateful for you, and I love you with all my heart.

As I've said many times, "The quality of my life is in direct proportion to the number and quality of the people in it." I'm truly a blessed man.

ABOUT THE AUTHOR

"I'M INSPIRED TO HELP OTHERS HAVE A BIG LIFE IN PURSUIT OF THEIR ULTIMATE BEST."

I'm an Atlanta native and a graduate of Georgia State University with a business degree. During college, when I was selling newspaper subscriptions door-to-door for the *Atlanta Journal-Constitution*, I started to realize what this diverse and exciting city had to offer. I also learned that the power of authentic connections and adding value to every conversation leads to amazing outcomes.

My early love of music inspired me to learn to play the guitar and chase rock stardom for close to a decade, but with marginal financial results and elevated life goals, I knew I had to make a radical change in direction. Newly married and with a baby on the way, it was time to move on from the music industry. In 1996, I cut my signature long hair and made the switch to real estate sales and marketing . . . and I've never looked back.

I'm a competitive person by nature, so in my first four years, I quickly grew my business as a top producing agent and was offered an investment opportunity—buying into the first Keller Williams office in Atlanta. Keller Williams Realty, known for its rich culture, training and coaching, opened my eyes to the concept of "building a company within a company" to create a dynamic and effective team. This commitment propelled my career to the next level.

Starting in 1999, I opened and bought into twelve Keller Williams offices and held the role of operating partner for eight locations over a span of twenty years. Additionally, I led my own team of realtors to the top five in the country for the company. These offices have continued to thrive. Last year alone, our group (The Heart of Atlanta Group for Keller Williams) sold approximately 12,000 homes with a total value exceeding $3.4 billion. This success placed us in the top fifty real estate office groups in the country for all companies. The leaders in our offices and our outstanding real estate agents don't settle for less than the best for our clients. Together, we've created a culture where sharing your best ideas and supporting each other is the norm. In everything we do, we succeed together.

In 2016, I merged teams with Marc Takacs and later joined forces with Pam Ahern to form the super group, RPM Home Advisors. Our amazing mix of talent virtually guarantees the best experience for our home buying and selling clients. In fact, we're obsessed with excellence.

When I'm not busy in the real estate world as a teacher and coach, I still play guitar in a great band, and I love to have adventures with my wife Pauline and our four adult sons: Cory, Alex, Tyler and Luke. I enjoy traveling, snowboarding, wakeboarding and scuba diving.

I'm also involved in numerous organizations that allow me to help at-risk kids and teens, including my favorite, Camp Grace, an organization committed to summer camp adventures for disadvantaged kids. My support for those who are less fortunate includes homeless shelters, affordable housing for single women with children, and educational non-profits to help people escape dependency and enjoy self-sufficiency. In my relationships with all of these people, I want to inspire the dreams of those that have lost sight of their potential.

Over the course of my career and in my personal life, I've had the privilege to meet some amazingly talented people. I wake up every day inspired to be a servant leader, knowing that my team and I are making a positive impact in the lives of those around us.

RESOURCES

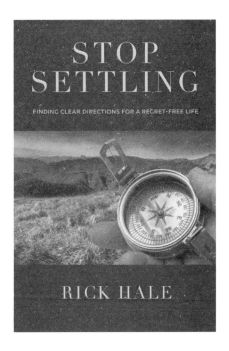

Stop Settling is available in casebound, ebook versions, and audio. To order, go to RickHale.com or Amazon.com

SPEAKING OPPORTUNITIES

Rick is available to speak to real estate companies, other businesses, leadership teams, civic groups, youth groups, and churches. To find out more and schedule an engagement, go to RickHale.com